MATHEMATICAL SNAPSHOTS DISCARD

Third American Edition, Revised and Enlarged

Mathematical Snapshots

H. STEINHAUS

With a New Preface by
MORRIS KLINE

OXFORD UNIVERSITY PRESS
Oxford   New York   Toronto   Melbourne

Oxford University Press

Oxford   London   Glasgow
New York   Toronto   Melbourne   Auckland
Delhi   Bombay   Calcutta   Madras   Karachi
Kuala Lumpur   Singapore   Hong Kong   Tokyo
Nairobi   Dar es Salaam   Cape Town

and associate companies in
Beirut   Berlin   Ibadan   Mexico City   Nicosia

Library of Congress Cataloging in Publication Data
Steinhaus, Hugo.
    Mathematical snapshots.
    Reprint. Originally published: 3rd American ed., rev.
and enl. Oxford, Oxfordshire;
New York: Oxford University Press, 1969.
    Includes bibliographical references and index.
    1. Mathematics — Popular works.
2. Mathematical recreations. I. Title.
QA93.S69   1983   510   82-22340
ISBN 0-19-503267-5 (pbk.)

Printing (last digit): 9 8 7 6 5 4 3

Printed in the United States of America

Preface to the Galaxy Edition

This reprinting of the third, enlarged edition of Steinhaus's *Mathematical Snapshots* is more than welcome.

The book must be distinguished from numerous books on riddles, puzzles, and paradoxes. Such books may be amusing but in almost all cases the mathematical content is minor if not trivial. For example, many present false proofs and the reader is challenged to find the fallacies.

Professor Steinhaus is not concerned with such amusements. His snapshots deal with straightforward excerpts culled from various parts of elementary mathematics. The excerpts involve themes of sound mathematics which are not commonly found in texts or popular books. Many have application to real problems, and Steinhaus presents these applications. The great merit of his topics is that they are astonishing, intriguing, and delightful. The variety of themes is large. Included are unusual constructions, games which involve significant mathematics, clever reasoning about triangles, squares, polyhedra, and circles, and other very novel topics. All of these are independent so that one can concentrate on those that attract one most. All are interesting and even engrossing.

Professor Steinhaus explains the mathematics and his fine figures and excellent photographs are immensely helpful in understanding what he has presented. He does raise some questions the answers to which may be within the scope of most readers but the reader is warned that some answers have thus far eluded the efforts of the greatest mathematicians. Mathematical proof demands more than intuition, inference based on special cases, or visual evidence.

This book should be and can be read by laymen interested in the surprises and challenges basic mathematics has to offer. Professor Steinhaus is mathematically distinguished, and, as evidenced by the very fact that he has undertaken to present unusual, though elementary, features, is seriously concerned with the spread of mathematical knowledge. The careful reader will derive pleasure from the material and at the same time learn some sound mathematics, which is as relevant today as when the original Polish edition was published in 1938.

MORRIS KLINE
*Professor Emeritus of Mathematics
at the Courant Institute
of Mathematical Sciences,*
New York University

November 1982

Foreword

In presenting this book to the reader, I should like to avoid the misunderstanding that any mathematician risks when he addresses himself to non-specialists. My purpose is neither to teach, in the usual sense of the word, nor to amuse the reader with some charades. One fine summer day it happened that I was asked this question: "You claim to be a mathematician; well, what does one do all day when one is a mathematician?" We were seated in a park, my questioner and I, and I tried to explain to him a few geometric problems, solved and unsolved, using a stick to draw on the gravel pathway a Jordan curve, or a Peano curve...That was how I conceived this book, in which the sketches, diagrams, and photographs provide a direct language and allow proofs to be avoided or at least reduced to a minimum.

H. Steinhaus

Contents

1

Triangles, Squares, and Games

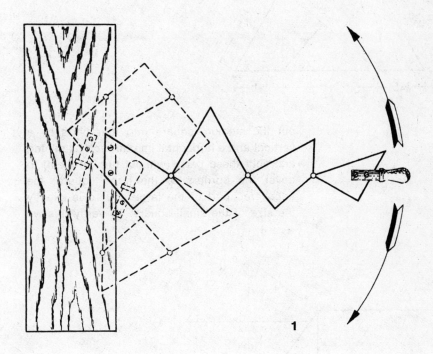

1

From these four small boards (1) we can compose a square or an equilateral triangle, according as we turn the handle up or down. The proof is given by sketch (2).

To decompose a square into two squares we draw a right triangle (3); to verify that the large square is the sum of the two others, we

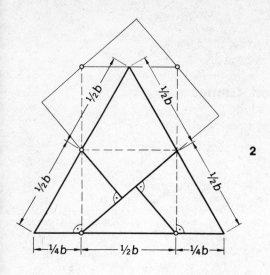

2

cut the medium square into four parts by a vertical and a horizontal line through its center, and shift these parts (without turning them) to cover the corners of the large square; the uncovered part of the large square is exactly the size of the small square. To verify this we

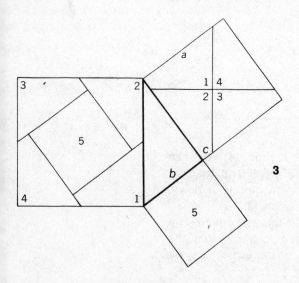

3

have only to remark that $a = b + c$. The meaning of the theorem thus proved is clear when we look at the triangle (**4**) with sides 3, 4, and 5: $9 + 16 = 25$. Thus we can draw a right angle by using a string 12 inches long with knots 3, 4, and 5 inches apart.

We may also verify this property of a right triangle without squares (**5**).

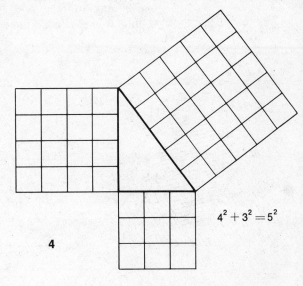

$$4^2 + 3^2 = 5^2$$

4

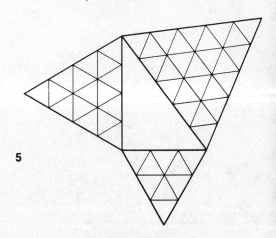

5

Let us draw equilateral triangles upon the sides of a given triangle *ABC*, one of whose angles (*C*) is equal to 60° (**6**). The combined area of the original *ABC* and of the new triangle opposite *C* is equal to the combined area of the remaining triangles. *Proof* (**7**): 1 + 2 + 3 = 1′ + 2′ + 3′.

To draw an equilateral triangle we can start with any triangle and trisect its angles: the little triangle in the middle is equilateral (**8**).

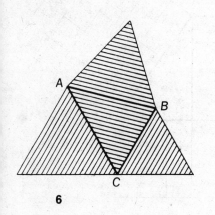

6

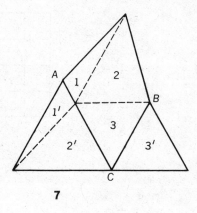

7

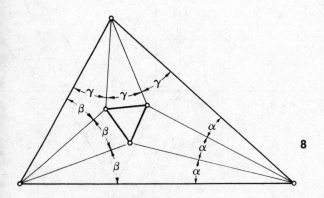

8

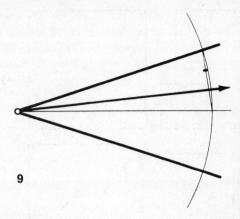

9

The trisection of an angle can be done very accurately by first halving it (**9**) and then dividing the chord of the half into three equal parts: the radius cutting 2/3 off the chord trisects the angle. This construction is only an approximate one.

It is easy to cover a plane with squares of different sizes (**10**). A very interesting problem is to divide a rectangle into squares, each of them different. On the following page they are

10

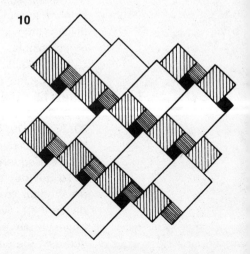

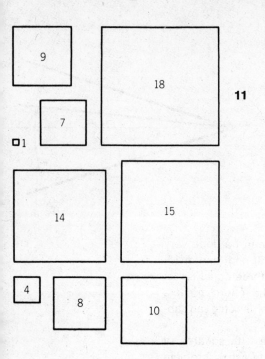

given (**11**), nine in number, with sides 1, 4, 7, 8, 9, 10, 14, 15, 18. *Problem*: form a rectangle with them. This is the simplest example of division of a rectangle into different squares. A division into fewer than nine different squares is impossible.

It is possible to divide a square into different squares. One of the simplest cases is drawn here (**12**). The sides of the 24 squares are: 1, 2, 3, 4, 5, 8, 9, 14, 16, 18, 20, 29, 30, 31, 33, 35, 38, 39, 43, 51, 55, 56, 64, and 81. Can a square be decomposed into fewer than 24 different squares?

To cut out of any triangle another with an area equal to one-seventh of the whole, we divide (**13**) every side in the ratio 1:2 and connect the points of division with opposite vertices; the shaded area in the middle is one-

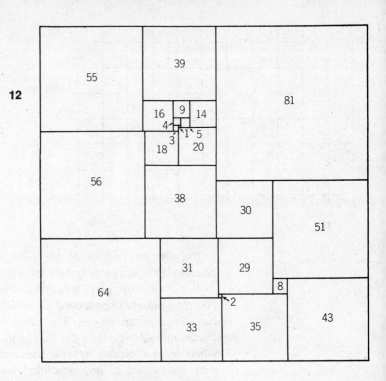

seventh of the whole and the proof is to be read from the adjoining figure (**14**): the black and the shaded parts give 7 congruent triangles, each equal to the shaded area; as the 6 black triangles can be used to cover the white parts, the 7 congruent triangles together give the great triangle.

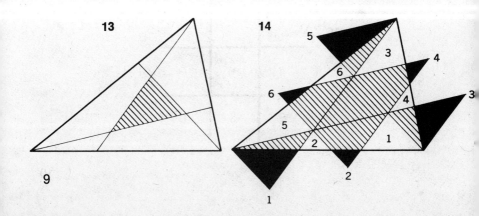

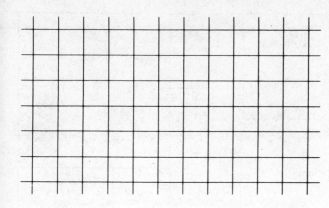

15

The simplest division of the plane, into equal squares (**15**), gives a board for many games. Two people can play 'three-in-a-row' on this (**16**) nine-square chessboard. One of the players has three white pieces, the other has three black ones. They place the pieces in turn, and when all six pieces are on the board, each may be moved to any adjoining square (but not diagonally). The one who first places his pieces in a horizontal, vertical, or diagonal row is the winner. The first player is sure to win if he at once occupies the center square and then plays sensibly. For, if White occupies *e*, Black can counter in only two ways: by

16

a	b	c
d	e	f
g	h	i

covering either a corner square or a side square between corners. If Black covers *a*, White ought to cover *h*, compelling Black to choose *b*, then White will have to cover *c*, causing Black to occupy *g*. Now White in the next two moves will pass from *e* to *f* and from *h* to *i* and win. If Black begins by choosing *b*, White will cover *g*, Black *c*, White *a*, Black *d*, and White will pass from *g* to *h* and then from *h* to *i*, moves that the black piece covering *c* will be unable to prevent. If the leader is not allowed to cover *e*, the game, if played cleverly by both partners, will degenerate to an endless repetition of identical cycles.

There are positions in chess that permit of an exact analysis. For example, the end-game of Dr. J. Berger (**17**) assures victory to White, provided White begins with the move *Q—QKt*8. He will not win if he begins with any other move, provided Black defends himself sensibly. But if White begins with the above-mentioned move and continues properly, in eight moves the game should become an evident win for him. Certain end-games are famous because of their cleverly hidden solutions. Although (**18**) is not of this class, it is by no means an easy task for the beginner to find out how White can checkmate in four moves at most.

18

19

Dr. K. Ebersz's end-game is of an entirely mathematical character (**19**). It can be proved rigorously that White will not allow Black's king to take any of his pawns, provided that he always moves to the square on which Black's king is then standing. He must therefore start by the move *B-F*. If he observes this rule, the game will end in a draw, but if he makes one false move, then Black can prevent him, if he chooses, from applying such tactics, and may break through *X-Y* or *O-O*. An interesting end-game would be one in which the moves of one player were exactly determined by those of his opponent, the game also ending in a draw, but the player who first departed from the rule would lose the game, provided his opponent played in a certain way that would also be fully determined.

There is no need for the reader to be a great chessplayer in order to secure in a simultaneous game against two chess champions *A* and *B* the result 1:1. It is only necessary that *A* play with white and *B* with black pieces, and *A* begin the game. The reader *R* repeats the first move of *A* on *B*'s chessboard, thus starting the play against *B*. After *B*'s countermove *R* transfers it as his answer against *A* on *A*'s chessboard. Thus on both chessboards the same game will be played. On the first chessboard the result for *R* can only be 1, 0, or 1/2 and on the second chessboard 0, 1, or 1/2. Thus in each case *R* wins one point (1 + 0, 0 + 1 or 1/2 + 1/2), while *A* and *B* together win only one point as well.

Under the rules of chess, Black wins when he is able to call 'Checkmate,' meaning that White's king cannot avoid capture on the next move. The game is a draw if it has reached a situation making victory impossible for either player. There is also a situation called 'pat,' which makes necessary a suicide for one of the kings. Our sketch (**20**) shows a position that cannot be classified as a victory, or as a draw, or as a pat. The last piece to be moved was the Black knight. It is now White's turn; but it is impossible for White to move.

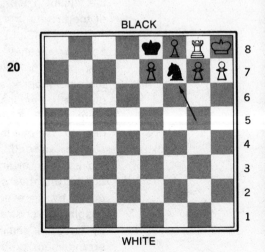

20

BLACK

WHITE

21

22

There is no mathematical theory of the game of chess, but there is one in certain simpler games. For example, in a box (**21**) there are 15 numbered tablets, and there is an empty space for one more. Lay the tablets in the box in any desired order (**22**) and then, by suitable moves, arrange them as they were originally ordered. The theory is as follows: let us call the vacant place '16'; then every arrangement of the tablets is a permutation of the numbers 1, 2, 3 . . . 15, 16. Now, by writing these numbers first in their natural order 1 . . . 16 and then appropriately interchanging them with their neighbors, every desired order can be obtained. For instance, to get the arrangement 2, 1, 3, 4, 5 . . . 16, one interchange is needed. We call it a move. Some arrangements require an odd, some an even number of moves. If an arrangement is to be reached by an odd number of moves, it is impossible to get it by an even number of moves. Let us imagine the contrary: an arrangement produced by an even number of moves and the same arrangement produced by an odd number of

14

moves. Starting with the natural arrangement, executing the even number of moves and then the odd number of moves but in the opposite direction, we should come back to the natural order. Thus in an odd number of moves we could pass from the natural order to itself. This is impossible because every move is an interchanging of two neighbors. Consider first only moves interchanging 5 with 6. The first move of this kind changes 56 into 65, the second one changes 65 into 56, and so on; as we must eventually re-establish the natural order 56, the number of the moves considered is even. The same reasoning applies to the pair 1-2, to the pair 2-3 . . . and to the pair 15-16: for every pair there is an even number of moves which interchanges it. Thus the total number of moves employed to pass from the natural order back to itself is even, being a sum of even numbers. Thus we can classify all arrangements into two classes: the 'even' and the 'odd' arrangements. Let us consider the arrangements of tablets in the box as an arrangement of numbers, reading them down line by line. When we shift the tablets in the box, we can only interchange the vacant place '16' with one of its neighbors. If this neighbor is the right or the left one, the interchanging is a 'move' in the previous sense, as if all the horizontal lines formed one line. If, however, we interchange the tablet '16' with its upper or lower neighbor, the step is equivalent to interchanging two tablets that, in the total line, have the distance 4. Such an interchange requires 7 moves, i.e. 7 interchangings of neighbors. To solve our problem, we must in any case bring the tablet '16' in the box back to its initial position in the bottom right-hand corner; it must be therefore shifted as many times to the left as to the right and as many times up as down. The number of horizontal shiftings is therefore an even number $2h$, and the number of vertical shiftings also an even number $2v$. The whole process is thus equivalent to $2h$ moves plus $2v \times 7$ moves $= 2h + 14v$ moves and this number is even. Consequently, if an arrangement is to be obtained from the basic one by an odd number of 'moves,' the problem of passing back is insoluble. For instance, we cannot, by moving the tablets, change the arrangement given on our illustration into that shown on the drawing of the box, nor can we pass from the first to the second one. (Why?) All arrangements that can be reached by an even number of 'moves' define soluble problems; the reader may try to prove this statement.

All the games mentioned here and many others have something in common. Not only the end-games of chess but also 'wolf and sheep' and 'three-in-a-row' have theories indicating which color (Black or White) will win, provided he plays properly. The theory teaches at the same time how to play properly. The case of a draw seems to be an exception but we can exclude it by the rule that the player who is confronted by a position that has previously occurred and who makes the same move a second time is defeated. Now, there is a general theorem to the effect that all games of the kind described above are either unfair or futile. We call a game *futile* if it permits a draw when properly played by both partners. In certain games no draw is possible; we call them *categorical*. In others we can exclude the draw by supplementary rules, as mentioned above. Our thesis affirms that all categorical games are unfair. The meaning of this thesis is that only one color has a method of winning whatever his opponent may do. To discover this method may be very easy, as in 'wolf and sheep,' or very difficult, as in some end-games of chess; nevertheless the existence of the winning color and of the winning method is certain. The theorem is general enough to apply also to such games as chess, provided it has been made categorical by the rule of repetition mentioned above and by considering as defeated a partner who gets into a 'rut.'

To prove the theorem, consider an end-game that assures a victory to White after 4 moves at most. Let us call it an EG_4. It is clear that there exists an initial move for White so that whatever Black's answer may be, the resulting position becomes an EG_3. Let us call this move a good one. White now has another good move, reducing the position to an EG_2, and so on, until an EG_1 is reached. There is now a victorious move for White: the checkmate. Of course, a wrong defense by Black can accelerate his defeat; instead of being checkmated after exactly 4 moves he may be so after 3 moves. In any case White has a series of good moves leading to victory in 4 moves or less. Now it is clear what an EG_n means. All EG_n's, where n is any natural number ($n = 1, 2, 3 \ldots$), are called victorious for White. Let us consider the initial position in chess, when all 32 pieces are ordered ready for the battle. Two cases are logically possible and mutually exclusive: (I) the position is victorious for White, (II) the position is not victorious for White. In the first case, the game of chess is essentially victorious for White: it is simply an EG_n. In the second case, the initial position is not an EG_n. In this case there exists for every definite move M of White an answer such that the resulting position is not an EG_n —in fact, if no such answer should exist, every answer would change the position into one victorious for White and, consequently, the initial position itself would be victorious for White, against our assumption. Thus we know that M can be answered by Black in a way that the resulting position is still not an EG_n. Applying the same argument to the new position, we see that Black can find an answer to any second movement M' of White's, leading to a 'not an EG_n.' As White can win only by getting an EG_1—which never will happen— and as the game is categorical, Black can win it, whatever White may do. We don't know which of the two cases, I or II, corresponds to the real modified chess, but we are sure that one and only one of them is true, a fact implying that chess is an unfair game. The same reasoning applies to checkers, halma, and many other games. If they are not categorical, they must be futile. We do not know whether ordinary (not modified) chess is futile or not. In the negative case we know that it is unfair, but we do not know which color is the privileged one. Even if we knew it, we should not necessarily have the knowledge of the winning method. If we knew that chess is futile, we could still be ignorant of the methods leading to a draw.

There are games of a different kind to which the theory advanced above does not apply. The same board used for the 'three-in-a-row' game can be used for the following one. The board (**23**) carries 9 numbers, some black and some white. White writes 0, 00, or 000 on a piece of paper and on another Black writes I, II, or III, but neither of them sees what his opponent writes. Then they produce the scraps and determine the column and the line on the board. The number found in the

23

	0	00	000
I	1	3	2
II	2	3	1
III	3	1	4

line and column gives the number of dimes
White is to get from his opponent, if it is
white, and the number he has to pay to Black,
if it is black. The peculiarity of this game consists in its not being 'closed.' To explain the
meaning of this remark, let us suppose that
White always chooses $\bigcap\bigcap$ and that Black has
already noticed this preference. The best Black
can do under such circumstances is to choose
$\|$; he will win three dimes by this method
in every run. Of course White will learn this
trick of Black by experience, and before long
he will find that he has to change his habit
and choose $\bigcap$. This policy will bring him two
dimes in every run, so long as Black keeps
to $\|$. It is easy to see that this mutual adapta-
tion never leads to a rigid method for either of
the partners. In chess the situation is different.
In Dr. Berger's end-game, the solution given
in our text* is the best for both partners. If
White knows that his opponent never makes
mistakes, he will begin with *Q—QKt8*; otherwise he could not expect a victory in his 13th
move. If Black knows his opponent is an ideal
player, he will answer by *B—QB5*; any different
move would enable White to checkmate him
before the 13th move. The contest will thus
continue according to the 'principal solution'
of our test. In such a play the two methods,
Black's and White's, are mutually best. The
existence of such 'principal solutions' makes
a game 'closed.' Chess is thus a closed game,
and all ordinary games like checkers, halma,
and so on which we have shown to be unfair
or futile are closed, whereas our new game

*See Note (17) at the end of the book.

of 9 squares is neither closed nor unjust; it is open and equitable like 'matching pennies.' Of course, the fact that in these games there is no first and no second player is essential.

Let a rabbit be locked up in a garden (24) separated by a fence from the street. The dog on the street is eager to approach as closely as possible to the rabbit, while the rabbit wants to keep clear of the barking aggressor. Each of them is in search of a point of vantage and estimates its value according to the mutual distance it guarantees, but for the rabbit this value increases with the distance whereas it decreases for the dog. Neither of them is a mathematician so they proceed by trial and error.

When the dog appears at 1 the rabbit retires to 1′; because of the semicircular shape of the back wall (C is the center of the circle) 1′ is the farthest point from 1. The best the dog

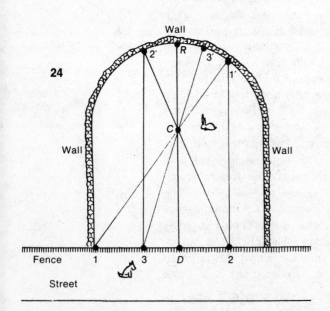

24

can do now is to run to point 2 which is the nearest to 1′ among all points accessible to the dog. Perceiving the dog at 2 the rabbit hastens to 2′; an obvious answer of the dog is to place himself in 3, etc. It is easily seen that the successive positions of the dog 1, 2, 3 . . . approach more and more the point D, while the positions of the rabbit 1′, 2′, 3′ . . . approach the point R. After a finite time (why?) the dog reaches D and the rabbit arrives at R, and both animals feel satisfied: the dog, because any movement of his would increase his distance from the rabbit in R; the rabbit, because any change of place would bring him nearer to the point D occupied by the dog. Calling d the distance DR we can say that the dog can play his game in a way to secure the distance d and that he cannot secure any distance $d′$ less than d; the rabbit can also play in a manner to secure the distance d but no distance $d′$ greater than d. The fact that both animals can be satisfied simultaneously is a proof for the closedness of the game. The position D, R is the solution of this game.

In a rectangular garden (25) things are quite different. Trying to do his best the dog occupies the middle D of the fence—it is obvious that this choice is the best possible, as it guarantees that the rabbit will not increase the distance beyond the length $D1$; any other choice than D (e.g. E) would imply the possibility of the rabbit's escaping farther away (e.g. to 2). The rabbit's answer is a flight to 1: this is best for him. This action is answered by the dog's running to 1′, which is the point nearest to 1. Naturally the next move of the rabbit brings him to 2, and, obviously, is followed by the dog's run from 1′ to 2′; the rabbit escapes to 1 and this hunting continues

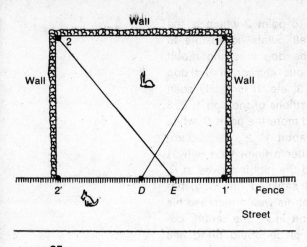

25

indefinitely. No stable solution exists, whatever the animals do: the game is open.

Let us consider two belligerent countries— call them '*N*(orth)' and '*S*(outh)' respectively. *N* produces two kinds of tanks—*A* and *B*; *S* has also two types—*C* and *D*. Now, the experience of many battles has proved that *A* wins over *C* in 60 per cent of encounters. *C* beats *B* in 80 per cent of fights, *B* wins over *D* in 70 per cent, and, finally, *D* wins in 60 per cent of battles when faced with *A*. The problem for *N* is to decide which type of tank has to be produced and which to be rejected; an analogous problem haunts *S*. It is easily seen that no solution of this kind is possible: If *N* chooses *A* then *S* chooses *D*; *N* seeing only *D* as his opponent halts the production of *A* and starts to produce *B* exclusively. This change induces *S* to produce only *C*, which in turn compels *N* go back to *A*. This will probably remind the reader of the sketch (**25**) where the dog and the rabbit never cease running to and fro.

Our present case is consequently an open game; now the reader may employ the theorem about the possibility of closing the game (by mixing the strategies). Therefore each party will do best to produce both types of tanks in an appropriate proportion: N must produce tanks A and B in the proportion 5:2, and S has to produce C and D in the proportion 3:4. The calculation shows that if N keeps to this rule the number of victories for him will be 48 per cent whatever S does; on the other hand, S obeying our counsel will be sure of winning 52 per cent of battles whatever N does. Consequently, the strategies recommended by us are mutually the best, and mixing the tanks as specified makes the war a closed game.

There is a legend to the effect that the Brahmin who invented chess demanded of the King of Persia as a reward as much wheat as would cover the whole chessboard, beginning by placing one grain on the first square, two on the next, and so on, always doubling the number of grains (**26**). It turned out that not only the Shah but all the granaries in the world put together would be unable to furnish so much wheat. The Brahmin demanded in a modest way

$$1 + 2 + 2^2 + \ldots + 2^{63} = 2^{64} - 1$$

grains. The number runs into 20 figures and has divisors. (What divisors?)

If we place two chessboards alongside each other, continuing the process from the first to the second chessboard, and take one grain from the last square of the second board, there will remain upon that square $p = 2^{127} - 1$ or

170 141 183 460 469 231 731
687 303 715 884 105 727

grains; this number has no divisors, it is a

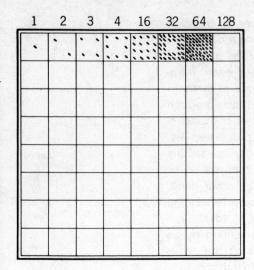

1	2	3	4	16	32	64	128

26

prime number, and has 39 figures. There is no difficulty in proving the existence of a still greater 39-digit prime number without exhibiting it. It has been established that the number $180p^2 + 1$ is also a prime number. Here it is:

$$5\ 210\ 644\ 015\ 679\ 228\ 794\ 060$$
$$694\ 325\ 391\ 135\ 853\ 335\ 898$$
$$483\ 908\ 056\ 458\ 352\ 201\ 854$$
$$618\ 372\ 555\ 735\ 221.$$

$2^{2281} - 1$ was found to be a prime by the SWAC electronic computer on 7 October 1952; it has 687 decimal figures. The 1332 figures of the prime number $2^{4423} - 1$ can be found in the April 1962 issue of *Recreational Math. Magazine*. In vol. 18 (1964), p. 13, of *Mathematics of Computation* the 3376 figures of the prime $2^{11213} - 1$ have been published; no greater primes have been made available since. The achievements quoted above would be scarcely possible without modern computing devices, whose capabilities are still far from fully explored.

We can carry out on a chessboard the following experiment: smear glue over the chessboard and sprinkle on it some grains. Repeat this until 64 grains appear on the chessboard. Obviously, not all squares contain the same number of grains; some are empty, others get only one grain, others again two, etc. The calculus of probability tells us to expect twenty-four squares to remain empty, twenty-four squares to contain one grain, twelve squares to contain two grains, three squares three grains, and one square four grains. (The exact computation gives fractional numbers of grains, so that the sum of the products equals 64 grains.)

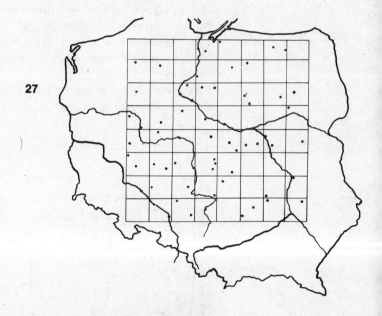

27

This experiment will show itself to be more remarkable when on the map of Poland (**27**) we draw a square divided in 64 fields and mark on this territory the 64 largest towns. As may be seen from the map, there are fewer empty squares and more squares containing only one town than we may expect from the computation above. This is due to the trend of towns to keep apart from one another: obviously district-towns will not be too near to each other. But choosing only the 16 largest Polish towns, the result is in good accordance with the theory of probability.

The same idea applies to the arrangement of chromosomes in certain human cells (leukocytes). Microphotography makes them visible and there are 46 in every such cell. Here we have to replace each chromosome by a point called the 'centromere,' the spot where the chromosome is narrowest. The 46 centromeres and a polygon serving as a frame drawn round the totality of chromosomes are transferred from the photo to a sketch (**28**) with a covering grid of squares, each square having an area equal to 1/46 of the polygon.

When speaking of the 64 towns (**27**) we had already appealed to the calculus of probability

28

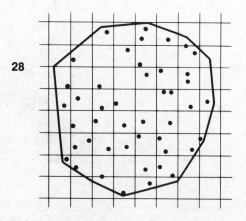

to tell us how many of the 64 squares to expect to be empty, how many to contain one town, and so on. Now we are challenged by the same problem with the 64 replaced by 46. Table I is interpreted as follows: we have to expect an average of 17.1 squares to contain one centromere, 8.55 squares to contain two, etc., and lastly, 16.73 squares to contain no centromeres.

Squares	$\boxed{\,\cdot\,}$	$\boxed{\cdot\,\cdot}$	$\boxed{\cdot\!\cdot\,\cdot}$	$\boxed{\cdot\cdot\,\cdot\cdot}$	Empty
Expected	17.1	8.55	2.79	0.83	16.73
Observed	27.0	7.1	1.06	0.02	10.88

Table I

The data of the second line were furnished by an empirical study of 50 leukocytes. The average number of squares occupied by single centromeres turned out to be 27. The difference 27 − 17.1 is big enough to show that the chromosomes do not move blindly; they tend to avoid proximity to one another, which behavior increases to 27 the average number of squares with a single inhabitant and diminishes almost to zero the number of squares with four or more centromeres.

So far we have described no example of sets of points arranged purely at random. The microscope has failed us, so we appeal to the telescope. From a field of stars in the constellation of Aquila we have employed all stars of magnitude 10-11 only. Moving a convex polygon over the star chart, we stopped when the polygon covered 46 stars (29). The example sought for is given in Table II, whose entries are almost identical with the expected numbers of Table I. This identity proves the random character of the distribution of the Aquila stars, as opposed to the behavior of chromosomes.

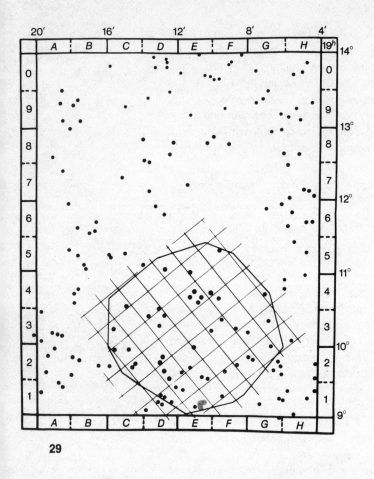

29

Squares	$\boxed{\cdot}$	$\boxed{\because}$	$\boxed{\therefore}$	$\boxed{\vdots}$	Empty
Observed	17	8	3	1	17

Table II

It is easy to write down very large numbers. Such giants can be defined very simply if we agree to write 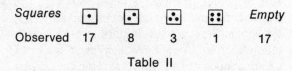 instead of a^a, $\boxed{a}$ instead of 'a in a triangles,' and $\text{\textcircled{$a$}}$ instead of 'a in a squares.' Then the number 'Mega' = $\text{\textcircled{2}}$ is

28

$$\text{MEGA} = \boxed{2} = \boxed{4} = \boxed{\triangle 2} = \boxed{\triangle 2^2} = \boxed{4^4} = \boxed{256} = \triangle 256 = \cdots$$

30

already too great to have any physical meaning (**30**), the last symbol being 256 in 256 triangles, and the reason why we have abandoned the ordinary system of writing numbers is clear. (The reader may try to explain the 'Megiston' given by (10)).

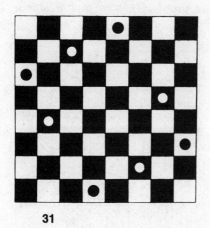

31

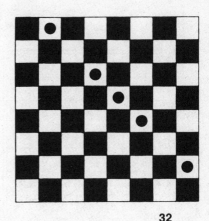

32

The chessboard has produced a great many puzzles and games. Thus we may place upon it eight queens (**31**) in such a way that none of them can attack any other. There are 92 different ways of so disposing the queens, all of which are obtainable from 12 fundamentally distinct arrangements, by suitable rotations and mirror reflections of the chessboard. It is possible to place five queens (**32**) on the chessboard so that each square will be attacked by at least one queen. There are 4860 solutions to this problem, and they may be obtained from 638 basically distinct ones. The problem may also be solved in such a way that the queens cannot attack each other. (How?)

Suppose some squares of the chessboard to be 'forbidden' to the king. They are chosen in such a manner as to prevent the king from reaching the right border of the chessboard if he starts anywhere on the left border. Then a rook can travel from the upper border to the lower one without leaving the forbidden squares. This property is shared by rectangular chessboards (with $m \times n$ squares); it is obvious but no simple proof is known to the author.

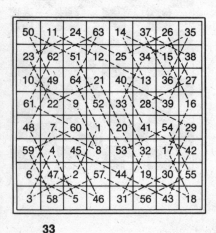

33

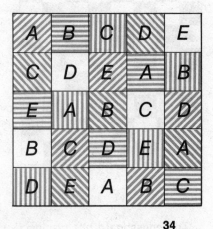

34

A knight may walk over the whole chessboard in 64 moves in such a way (**33**) that the polygon thus formed will have its center in the center of the chessboard, and the consecutive numbers of the squares will form a 'semi-magic square,' that is, their sum, in each column and in each row, will be equal (= 260; no other sum is possible; why?).

The great mathematician Euler was interested in this 'knight's tour' and other similar problems, e.g. that of the '36 officers.' This last problem is as follows: How is a delegation of six regiments, each of which sends a colonel, a lieutenant-colonel, a major, a captain, a lieutenant, and a sub-lieutenant, to be placed so that neither in any row nor in any file will regiment or officers' rank be repeated? This problem is impossible but we shall easily place 25 officers in the desired order (**34**): the shades stand for the regiments' colors and the letters for ranks.

These so-called Graeco-Latin squares can be applied for practical purposes. To study the influence of different treatments on different varieties of a plant we can divide a field into 25 plots (**35**) and denote by capital letters A, B, C, D, E five different varieties; the small letters g, h, i, j, l represent five different fertilizers. The arrangement exhibits in 25 plots the 25 possible combinations of 5 varieties with 5 fertilizers. If the rows have different degrees of humidity, our arrangement shows the combination of all varieties with every degree of humidity. For instance, the lowest degree of humidity r_1 appears combined with $A, B, C, D,$ and E, and the same is true of all degrees $r_2, r_3, r_4,$ and r_5. Moreover, the humidity r_1 appears combined with all fertilizers and the same is true for all degrees. The columns correspond to different systems of cultivation: it is obvious that the first column k_1 appears combined with all varieties, with all fertilizers, and with all humidities; the same is true of any other column. We have two systems of diagonals: m, n, p, q, t and u, v, w, x, y. The first system corresponds to five different times of sowing, the second to five different times of reaping. Let us consider the diagonal m: it

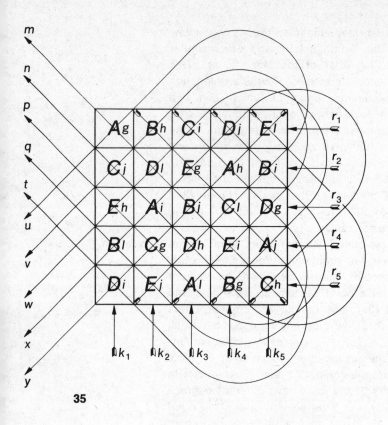

35

crosses every row, every column, its plots carry all the capital letters, of the group $g-l$, and all letters of the system $u-y$. Thus, if we compute the average yield m of the five plots m, we can expect to have eliminated all influences of treatment and of variety except the influence of the date of sowing. If we compute the average yield A of the five plots designated by this letter, we have eliminated all influences except the influence of variety. These statements, which result immediately from the inspection of the Graeco-Latin square, lead to the following method. Let M be the average yield per plot, i.e. the total yield divided by 25; let us designate, as above, by a letter the average yield of the plots corresponding to that letter, i.e. the sum of the five yields of the corresponding plots divided by 5. It is possible now to compute the following sum:

$$(M - A)^2 + (M - B)^2 + (M - C)^2 + (M - D)^2 + (M - E)^2$$

and analogous sums for other groups of letters:

$$(M - g)^2 + (M - h)^2 + (M - i)^2 + (M - j)^2 + (M - l)^2, (M - r_1)^2 + (M - r_2)^2 + (M - r_3)^2 + (M - r_4)^2 + (M - r_5)^2,$$

and so on.

The next step is to compare these sums. If, for instance, the first sum is greater than the second, we are entitled to the inference that the influence of the variety on the yield is greater than the influence of the fertilizer. The exact analysis of variances—this is the name of the method—is, however, more sophisticated: it also considers the question whether the differences of the sums are large enough not to be attributed to random deviations.

To win at horseracing it is not sufficient only to know the horses; we must know the betting people too. Staking on a very well-known horse one may, in the best case, win a little or nothing at all, because the majority of racegoers have had the same mind. Thus, one should choose a good horse whose merits are known only to a small number of bidders. The following game which can be played without horses or any gadgets belongs to the same kind. Persons in a room are each asked to deposit a dollar as a stake and to write separately on scraps of paper what they consider to be the height of the room. The scraps of paper are then gathered and the mean value of the guesses is computed. The man whose estimation comes nearest to this mean value gets all the money at stake. The point is that the room does not have to be measured at all, thus the owner of the apartment who knows the exact height has no greater chance than his rivals. In this game the knowledge of men is of no less importance than in the case of horsebetting.

1	~~2~~	3	4	5	6	7	8	9	~~10~~
~~11~~	12	13	14	15	16	17	18	19	20
21	22	23	24	25	26	27	28	29	30
31	32	33	34	35	36	37	38	39	40
41	42	43	44	45	46	47	48	49	~~50~~
51	52	53	54	55	56	~~57~~	58	59	60
61	62	63	64	65	66	67	68	69	70
71	72	73	74	75	76	77	78	79	80
81	82	83	84	85	86	87	88	89	90

36

A ticket (**36**) is divided into 90 rectangular fields, each of them labeled by a number; reading them as if it were a text we encounter all numbers from 1 to 90 in natural order. Some years ago there were in some European countries lotteries selling such tickets for a fixed price: the buyer had to scratch five of the 90 numbers (e.g. 2, 10, 11, 50, 57), leave a copy with the selling agent, and read next Sunday in a newspaper which five of ninety numbers were drawn in the lottery office. This office had to transfer 40 per cent of the money received to the housing fund (or other social project); the 60 per cent left was then divided into four equal parts: one part to be divided equally among tickets with five scratches agreeing with the five numbers drawn, another part equally among tickets with four agreeing scratches, another among such with three right guesses, and the last part among tickets with two right scratches. Let us call first prize (I) the money paid to the player with 5 right guesses on his ticket; second prize (II) is paid to each player who has 4 correct guesses, third (III) for 3, and fourth (IV) for 2 guesses. The reader may prove that prize I surpasses prize II, II surpasses III and III brings more money to the player than IV. The writer of this book was asked by several players why the numbers of tickets winning the II prize were, on ten consecutive Sundays, 21, 93, 1, 1, 4, 11, 5, 12, 1, 1. The newspapers published each Sunday the total number of tickets taking part in the game that week, and some players could determine by the calculus of probability the expected number of second prize tickets every week; because of fluctuations of the total numbers of tickets the expected number in question varied between 7.7 and 9. How to reconcile these limits with the ten figures above?

The answer has been given by a model (**37**) visualizing the results of a statistical inquiry based on 4000 old tickets supplied by the lottery office. Let us imagine these tickets as a pack and punch it with 90 vertical pins; the lengths of pins above the pack are proportional to the numbers of scratches placed on 4000 fields pierced by the pin in question. The reader can see a distinct predilection for central fields. If there was no such bias each pin would represent 222 scratches approximately; in reality, pin number 1 represents 119 scratches, number 90 has been scratched 127 times, 80 represents 98, but number 46 with 379 tickets scratched is the champion.

This startling phenomenon belongs to psychology: an irrational prejudice, shared by the

37

majority of gamblers, tells them that chance prefers the central fields. Their unconscious reason is perhaps the allegory of Fortune's arrow directed to the center of the target.

The real consequences of such irrational behavior are as follows: If the numbers drawn by the office of the mutual betting company are among those favored by the majority of players, the winners will be poorly rewarded in comparison with the prizes waiting for players preferring numbers repudiated by this majority. The probabilities of winning are the same in both cases, but the expected individual gain is significantly greater for the player belonging to the minority. Thus the model (37) can be employed by players free of prejudices: such players have only to scratch numbers indicated by short pins.

It has been proved experimentally that a player obeying the advice given above during several months wins enough to cover the price of tickets, which enables him to wait patiently for a significant profit; nonetheless it is unusual to meet such gamblers.

It would be possible to improve essentially the theory sketched here, by employing an electronic computer which could find out from old tickets the frequencies of pairs, triples, quadruples and quintuples.

The great mistake of the ordinary player is the desire to guess the numbers which will be drawn next Sunday, instead of collecting old tickets in order to see how to avoid on his own blank ticket those fields scratched frequently by other people.

The remarks above do not apply to lotteries promising fixed prizes.

To show the results of a real game played ten years ago and involving 1,371,127 tickets, and to compare the actual and the expected results, we oppose the numbers of winning tickets in the real game to the expected numbers of such tickets as furnished by the calculus of probability:

Prizes	I	II	III	IV
Actual numbers of winning tickets	0	117	4733	64451
Expected numbers of winning tickets	0.3	13.26	1114	30814

The example above shows that the five numbers drawn blindly happened to form a pattern popular with many players. They were dissatisfied, especially the winners of second prize, whose individual rewards were nine times smaller than the sum expected.

2

Rectangles, Numbers, and Tunes

Let us use the word *normal* for a rectangular sheet of paper that folded into two rectangular halves gives a sheet similar to the original one (**38**). Denoting its sides by a and b, we have the proportion $a : b = b : a/2$. Let us take two identical normal sheets and glue the base b of the second one to the long side a of the first (**39**). We get thus a great rectangle with sides $a + b$, b (the shaded part of the drawing) and a small rectangle with sides b, $a - b$ (the white part of the drawing). The proportion $a : b = b : a/2$ gives $a^2 = 2b^2$, making it easy to verify the proportion $a + b : b = b : a - b$. Thus the shaded rectangle is similar to the white one. Now the doubly shaded part is congruent to the white rectangle. Let us call the

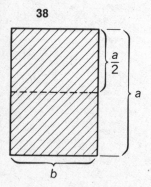

38

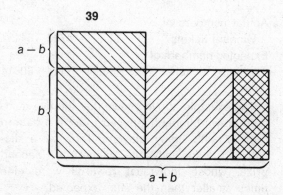

39

shape of the shaded rectangle hyper-normal; we have proved that by cutting off two squares of a hyper-normal sheet the remainder is still hyper-normal. Now let us suppose that we have a normal sheet with sides equal to a inches and b inches respectively, a and b being whole numbers. Of such a sheet we can make a hyper-normal one, as already seen; its sides will be whole numbers, when measured in inches: let us say p for the number of inches of the large and q for the number of inches of the small side. By cutting off two squares, we get a new hyper-normal sheet; its sides will be q and $p - 2q$ inches respectively. It is evident that these numbers are integers and that the new long side is less than half of the old long side. Proceeding in this manner, we get smaller and smaller hyper-normal sheets; after p steps we still ought to have a sheet with sides expressed in whole numbers when measured in inches—which is absurd because we lose at least one inch at every step and the long side must eventually disappear. This fact proves that there are no normal sheets with integer sides. It does not matter which units we choose: the argument holds for microns as well as for inches. The ratio of the sides of a normal sheet is $\sqrt{2}$, which means a number that multiplied with itself gives 2. What we have shown is that $\sqrt{2}$ is irrational, i.e. that it is not a ratio of two integers a/b.

We can show our result on the 'lattice of integers' (**40**). This is simply an array of points in rows and files at equal intervals like hop-poles or like the vertices of the squares of a chessboard extending over the whole plane. Placing the corner of a normal sheet over the lower left corner of the lattice and drawing the diagonal of the sheet, we get the oblique

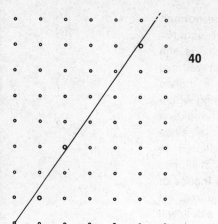

straight line. When we look along this line, we see not one hop-pole. (Why?)

The number $\sqrt{2}$ may also be expressed thus:

$$1 + \cfrac{1}{2 + \cfrac{1}{2 + \cfrac{1}{}}}$$

. . . . .

Calling this fraction x, we have as the first denominator the number $1 + x$, which implies that

$$x = 1 + \frac{1}{1 + x}, \quad x - 1 = \frac{1}{1 + x},$$

$$x^2 - 1 = 1, \quad x^2 = 2, \quad x = \sqrt{2}.$$

Hence approximate values of $\sqrt{2}$ are 1, 3/2, 7/5, 17/12 . . . The slope of the oblique line is $\sqrt{2}$; the fractions 1, 3/2 . . . give certain points of the lattice. For instance, 3/2 determines the point found by going 3 intervals up and 2 intervals to the right of the corner; we see these points approaching more and more closely the oblique line.

As we have shown already that $\sqrt{2}$ is not a ratio of two integers, a/b, we know that we cannot find integers a, b such as to have $a^2 = 2b^2$. In other words, given two equal detachments of soldiers forming two squares, it is impossible to make one square of them. However, it is possible to satisfy this whim if we do not care about one soldier more or less. The fractions already found give the following quadratic arrangements:

$$2^2 + 2^2 = 3^2 - 1, \quad 5^2 + 5^2 = 7^2 + 1,$$
$$12^2 + 12^2 = 17^2 - 1 \ldots$$

To get all the fractions needed we can start with 1/1 : the sum $1 + 1 = 2$ gives the next denominator, the sum $1 + 2 = 3$ gives the numerator, $3 + 2 = 5$ is the third denominator, $2 + 5 = 7$ the third numerator, and so on.

$$\frac{1}{1} \quad \frac{3}{2} \quad \frac{7}{5} \quad \frac{17}{12}$$

The arithmetical rule is as follows: if p/q is one fraction and P/Q the next, we have

$$Q = p + q, \quad P = q + Q = p + 2q.$$

Let us suppose that the fraction p/q gives a quadratic arrangement with one soldier more or less:

$$p^2 - 2q^2 = \pm 1;$$

we can easily show that P/Q is such an arrangement too. In fact, we have

$$\begin{aligned} P^2 - 2Q^2 &= (p + 2q)^2 - 2(p + q)^2 \\ &= p^2 + 4pq + 4q^2 - 2p^2 - 4pq - 2q^2 \\ &= 2q^2 - p^2 \\ &= \mp 1. \end{aligned}$$

Now 1/1 is obviously a solution:

$$1^2 - 2 \cdot 1^2 = -1;$$

then it follows that the next fraction is a solution too, and so on; all of the fractions are solutions and yield quadratic arrangements. We have stated this fact previously, but now we have a proof.

The method of our reasoning reminds us of playing with dominoes: (41) they are all standing in a file, and striking the first piece makes (42) all the other pieces fall. To foresee what will happen we have only to know that the first piece will be struck and that the pieces are standing so close that the fall of any piece implies the fall of the next piece. Such reasoning is called *mathematical induction*.

41

42

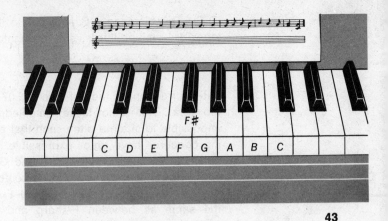

43

Rational and irrational numbers are connected with the problem of the musical scale (**43**). We call irrational those numbers that, like √2, are not expressible by a ratio *a/b* of two integers. In the scale C major (**44**) the intervals C-D, D-E, F-G, G-A, A-B must be equal ('whole tone'), while the intervals E-F and B-C are only a half of the former ones ('semitone').

44

The simplest concords have long since been examined on the monochord, and it has been found that the smaller the numbers expressing the relative frequency of the vibrations, the better the concord. High C has twice as many vibrations per second as low c, hence the octave is expressed by the ratio 2:1. The ratio 3:2 gives the fifth (C-G), 4:3 the fourth (C-F), 5:4 the major third (C-E), 6:5, the minor third

(D-F). The distance c-C is equal to 12 semi-tones $= 4$ minor thirds, so we ought to have

$$(6/5)^4 = 2;$$

but the fraction on the left side is 2.074, hence too great. This is not to be remedied, for it is impossible to attain a pitch such that all resulting concords have ratios expressible as ratios of whole numbers. Between F and G lies F-sharp (the black key in the very center of the octave); the ratio between C and F-sharp is the same as between F-sharp and high C, amounting to an augmented fourth. If we call x the ratio F-sharp : C, we get $x^2 = 2$, hence $x = \sqrt{2}$, which is an irrational number. The piano has a tempered scale; all the semitone intervals are equal to $^{12}\sqrt{2}$ but the concords are not exact. The violinist, following his musical sense, differs from the piano: for him the augmented fourth is 7:5 (he recedes from the tempered fourth just as does the point 7/5 on the lattice from the oblique straight line).

Let us divide the musical scale into 6, 7, 8, 9, etc. intervals (i.e. keeping to the principle of the tempered scale as explained above). To achieve a scale containing the natural concords with sufficient exactness we must proceed as far as a tempered scale of 19 tones. This can be seen on the sketch (45). The positions of the natural concords (the octave, the fifth, the fourth etc.) appear as verticals on (45). A piano having 19 keys instead of 12 would still be practicable and would have not only the advantage of better harmony, but would also have, for instance, different tones for C-sharp and D-flat, which are always distinguished in notes but not on the ordinary keyboard. These nuances correspond to the composer's intentions and in fact are respected by violinists.

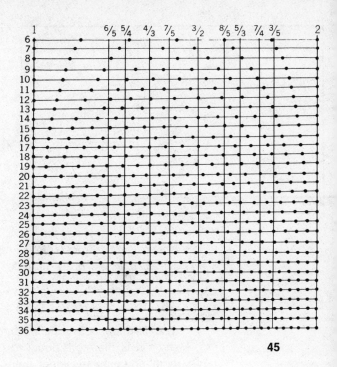

The infinite continued fraction giving $\sqrt{2}$ is not the simplest one; obviously

$$1 + \cfrac{1}{1 + \cfrac{1}{1 + \cfrac{1}{1}}}.$$

is the simplest possible. The number x given by this fraction is irrational. As we see beneath the first numerator 1 the fraction itself as denominator, we get

$$x = 1 + \frac{1}{x}, \quad x^2 - x = 1, \quad x = \frac{1}{2}(\sqrt{5} + 1).$$

Let us use the name 'golden rectangle' for a rectangular sheet that (**46**) is composed of a

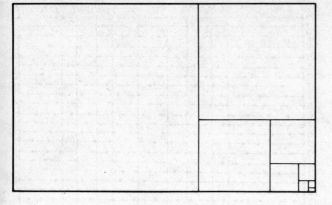

square and a rectangle similar to the whole sheet. If a and b are its sides, we get

$$a : b = b : a - b, \quad a^2 - ab = b^2,$$
$$(a/b)^2 - (a/b) = 1.$$

The fraction a/b satisfies the same equation as x: it is therefore equal to $(\sqrt{5} + 1)/2$. This number being irrational there are no integers a, b able to give a golden rectangle. We can, however, proceed as with $\sqrt{2}$; by terminating the continued fraction at various stages, we get successively

$$1/1, \ 2/1, \ 3/2, \ 5/3, \ 8/5, \ 13/8, \ldots$$

The fractions approach more and more the true value of the golden ratio, which is $1.618\ldots$ The numerators 1, 2, 3, 5, 8, 13, 21,... are the so-called Fibonacci numbers. These numbers are generated by successive addition, beginning with $1 + 1$:

$$1 + 1 = 2, \quad 1 + 2 = 3, \quad 2 + 3 = 5,$$
$$3 + 5 = 8, \quad 5 + 8 = 13, \quad \ldots$$

The nth number of the Fibonacci sequence is

$$\frac{1}{\sqrt{5}}\left\{\left(\frac{\sqrt{5} + 1}{2}\right)^n - \left(\frac{-\sqrt{5} + 1}{2}\right)^n\right\}$$

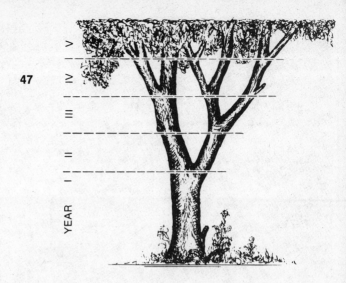

V
IV
III
II
I

YEAR

We could prove it by mathematical induction. (How?) If a tree (**47**) puts forth a new branch after one year, and always rests for a year, producing a new branch only in the following year, and if the same law applies to each branch, then in the first year we should have only the trunk, in the second, two branches, in the third, three, then 5, 8, 13, etc., as in Fibonacci's sequence.

This courtyard's sides (**48**) approximately observe the 'golden ratio.' The golden division of a segment is such that the whole has the same ratio to the greater part as the greater part to the smaller one: both ratios are then golden. (Why?)

We can decompose the golden rectangle into an infinite number of squares, marking first the greatest square possible in the rectangle (**46**), and proceeding similarly with the remaining rectangle, which is a golden rectangle, too, and so on. This geometrical procedure leads, when translated into arithmetic,

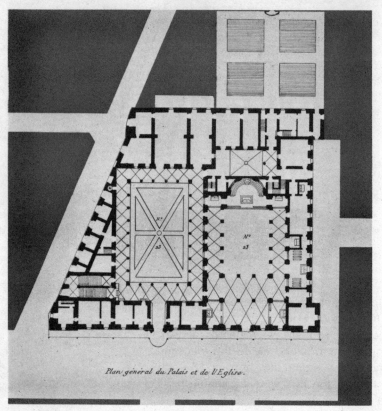

Plan général du Palais et de l'Eglise.

48

to the infinite continued fraction composed of unities, with which we started.

As can be seen from the sketch (**46**) the corners of the squares lying within the great rectangle form two straight lines: one being the diagonal of the great rectangle, the other the diagonal of the rectangle which still remains after cutting the square off. (Why?)

The consecutive multiples g, $2g$, $3g$ . . .

of the golden number $g = \dfrac{\sqrt{5} - 1}{2} = 0.618\ldots,$

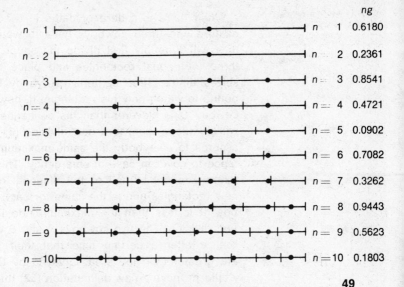

or rather their fractional parts, exhibit a certain uniformity not shared by the multiples of other fractions $(1-g$ excepted). The sketch **(49)** shows the division of the unit into 1, 2, 3 ... etc. parts. Let us look at the parts got by its division into five equal parts, for instance, and let us ascertain whether every part contains exactly one of the first five multiples of the golden number. This happens to be true but it is amazing that this uniformity applies to the whole sketch $(n = 1, 2, 3 ... 10)$ with only three failures against 52 successes. The deep reason for this phenomenon holding for almost all multiples of g is to be sought in the mysterious formula

$$\frac{\sqrt{5}-1}{2} = \cfrac{1}{1+\cfrac{1}{1+\cfrac{1}{1.}}}$$

When there is a herd of cattle in a square pasture and three cowboys have to watch it, they will probably first divide the square into three **(50)** equal rectangles and place themselves in the three centers, everybody being bound to watch only his rectangle. If, however, cowboy *C* is cleverer than his colleagues, he will persuade them to a new division **(51)** that assures to everybody the same maximum distance to cover in case of emergency. This distance is equal to half of the diagonal of the new rectangles and is the same for each cowboy; it is less than the maximum ride in the first division. The two cowboys *A* and *B* would realize after a certain time that their areas are greater than the area surveyed by *C* and would propose a new delimitation **(52)** that will neither change their positions nor affect the length of the maximum ride, but only satisfy the fair condition of every point being entrusted to the man who is nearest to it. *B*, dissatisfied with the new covenant because of the unequal distribution of the areas, which is still favorable to *C*, proposes an augmentation **(53)** of the area belonging to *C*, without changing the positions and the maximum rides. This plan having been accepted, *A* remarks that his principle of the nearest man has been violated.

50

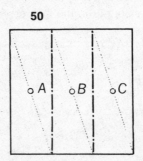

51

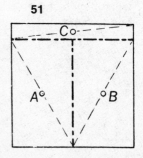

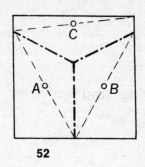
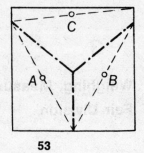
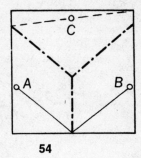

52   **53**   **54**

C replies that it can be saved if *A* and *B*
change their positions **(54)** without changing
the frontiers. This having been done, *A* and *B*
discover that they are wronged, because their
maximum ride is now longer than *C*'s. Finally
they agree to resume the first division into
equal rectangles.

3

Weighing, Measuring, and
Fair Division

Let us return for one moment to the chessboard. The first row is covered with 1, 2, 4
..., 128 grains. On the first and second square
together there are 3 grains, on the first and
third 5, on the second and third 6 grains, etc.;
it is possible to obtain every number from 1 to
255 by choosing appropriate numbers of the
series 1, 2, 4 ... 128 and summing up; no
more than 8 terms are needed.

We need only four weights (**55**) to make
every weight from 1 to 40, if we are allowed
to place them on both arms of the scale. This
corresponds to the development of numbers
in the ternary system, taking 3 as the radix. All
numbers from -40 to 40 (0 excepted) can be
thus written as $\pm 27 \pm 9 \pm 3 \pm 1$, using one
or more of the four numbers 1, 3, 9, 27. This
solves the puzzle of the 'girls' names': We
write down 80 different feminine names and
give them numbers from -40 to 40. Four cards
are signed *brunette, blonde, auburn,* and *red*;
one side of each card is labeled *black eyes,*
the other *blue eyes.* We will read 'brunette' as
27, 'blonde' as 9, 'auburn' as 3, 'red' as 1,
'black' as *plus,* and 'blue' as *minus.* Now if
for instance, Mabel has the number -25, we
have $-25 = -27 + 3 - 1$ and thence the
name Mabel must be written three times: on
the card of brunettes on the blue side, on the

card of the auburns on the black side, and on the cards of reds on the blue side. Someone who does not know the trick is given the cards and is told to think of a name and to find out the possible hues of hair and eyes. If he thinks of Mabel he will answer: She can be a brunette with blue eyes, an auburn with blue eyes, or a redhead* with black eyes. The man with the catalogue of names computes mentally $-27 - 1 + 3 = -25$ and finds the name Mabel.

1	= 1
2	= 3 − 1
3	= 3
4	= 3 + 1
5	= 9 − 3 − 1
6	= 9 − 3
7	= 9 − 3 + 1
8	= 9 − 1
9	= 9
10	= 9 + 1
11	= 9 + 3 − 1
12	= 9 + 3
13	= 9 + 3 + 1
14	= 27 − 9 − 3 − 1
15	= 27 − 9 − 3
16	= 27 − 9 − 3 + 1
17	= 27 − 9 − 1
18	= 27 − 9
19	= 27 − 9 + 1
20	= 27 − 9 + 3 − 1
21	= 27 − 9 + 3
22	= 27 − 9 + 3 + 1
23	= 27 − 3 − 1
24	= 27 − 3
25	= 27 − 3 + 1
26	= 27 − 1
27	= 27
28	= 27 + 1
29	= 27 + 3 − 1
30	= 27 + 3
31	= 27 + 3 + 1
32	= 27 + 9 − 3 − 1
33	= 27 + 9 − 3
34	= 27 + 9 + 1 − 3
35	= 27 + 9 − 1
36	= 27 + 9
37	= 27 + 9 + 1
38	= 27 + 9 + 3 − 1
39	= 27 + 9 + 3
40	= 27 + 9 + 3 + 1

55

When we have to compare objects on a scale without balance-weights, we can tell only which of the two is the heavier one. The question arises how to do it when we have more objects than two and we are allowed only to compare them pairwise. It is easy to find the heaviest one by comparing first a pair, then the heavier one with a third object, the heavier of the two with the fourth, and so on. For *n* objects we

56

57

58

need thus $n - 1$ steps. It is the same with tennis tournaments: to determine the best among n players, $n - 1$ matches are sufficient. Fewer than $n - 1$ are not sufficient. In fact, the best player has to be compared directly (by the result of a match) or indirectly (by the results of a chain of matches) with every other player. If we represent players as points and matches as lines joining the points, the winner must be connected with every other player by a system of lines and thus all the n points will be connected. Now it is easy to see (**56**) that we need at least $n - 1$ lines to connect n points. We can prove that fact by induction: we certainly need one line to connect two points; if we need $n - 1$ lines to connect n points and we have to adjoin a $(n + 1)$th point, the new point must certainly be connected by a new line to one of the old points and that step gives n lines as necessary. The tournaments are usually played by the cup method: players are grouped pairwise, the winners of the first round form new pairs—which gives the second round and so on until the final match gives the decision. So, for instance, if we have (**57**) 8 players, there are 4 matches in the first round, 2 in the second, and 1 in the third round, 7 matches in all; it is impossible to diminish this number, as we have already proved. Now, there is a custom to give the second prize to the finalist, i.e. to the player who has lost in the last round. This system is obviously unjust, because this player has not been compared with the players B and C who were beaten only by the first-prize winner and thus were eliminated before the last round. The number of these players is 3 in a tournament of 8. An additional tournament, requiring two matches, (**58**) is necessary to determine the best of three.

Generally, to determine the two best players among n contestants, $n - 1 + [\log_2(n - 1)]$ matches are enough. It has been proved that no smaller number is generally sufficient. 'Generally' means here that no method of determining the two best players is available that works in all cases with a smaller number of matches than the number given above. The fact that it can happen by accident that A beats B, B beats C, C beats D, and so on, so that after $n - 1$ matches we have determined not only the first- and second-best player but also the whole classification, $A, B, C \ldots N$ is not an argument for the chain method as described here, and against the cup method with an additional tournament; it shortens the procedure only because the players were listed by chance according to their ability.

To rank all objects by weighing them pairwise (and the same with ranking players by matches) we can adopt the following procedure: Let us suppose that we have already ranked a set of objects and we have to find a place among them for a new one. (**59**) We

59

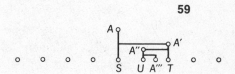

seek first the median, i.e. the object S which has as many objects above it as beneath it— if the number of objects is even, we call both objects in the middle of the range medians. Then we compare the new object A with the median; if it turns out to be heavier, we compare it with the median T of the upper half, if it is lighter, with the median of the lower half of the range, and so on, until it finds its place A''' between two neighbors U and T of the range. Let us begin with two objects; to rank them, one weighing is sufficient, to rank a third, two weighings at most are necessary; to place a fourth object among three already ranked, we compare it with the median—then, if it is heavier with the heaviest one and if lighter with the lightest one: that makes two steps. Thus we get the following sequence:

To place a new object among

1	2	3	4	5	6	7	. . . already ranked objects
1	2	2	3	3	3	3	. . . new weighings are suffi-

cient. Thus to rank

1	2	3	4	5	6	7	8	9	10	11	12	objects
0	1	3	5	8	11	14	17	21	25	29	33	. . .

weighings are sufficient. Nevertheless it is not the best method: the formula guarantees 8 weighings for 5 objects but 7 are sufficient. (How?)

The formula for n objects is

$$1 + kn - 2^k, \text{ where } k = 1 + [\log_2 n].$$

The number k alone has been shown to be sufficient for $n = 3, 4, 5, 6, 7, 8, 9, 10, 11$ as number of weighings; for $n = 12$ the formula gives $k = 29$; it has been proved that 29 weighings are not sufficient for 12 objects; 30 weighings, however, are sufficient.

This method has its significance not only in the classification of players and teams, but also in the ranking of any objects (for instance: cards in an alphabetic card index).

Our method of weighing reminds us of a problem of gunnery (**60**). There is a tank emplaced on a highway and the observer reports

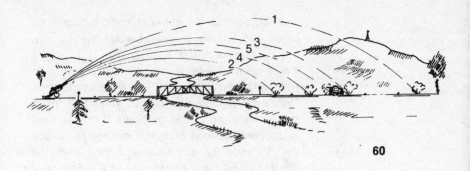

60

on which segment of the road it is situated. The gunner can hit any point of the segment he chooses, but the effect of the shot is reported to him by the observer only in terms of 'before' or 'beyond' the target. How should he proceed? If he shoots first to the midpoint of the segment, then to the midpoint of the first half if he was told 'beyond,' and to the midpoint of the second half if he was told 'before,' and continues to halve the segments, he will do best. The maximum distance between the target and the best shot among the n first shots is $L/2^n$, L being the length of the segment. This worst result happens only if the tank stands on one of the endpoints of the segment. The whole problem can be considered as a game. If the enemy knows the method of the gunner, he can place his tank so as to keep as far as possible from the n first shells. If this method is that of 'halving,' the enemy can do nothing better than to occupy one of the endpoints: this procedure gives him the margin of security $L/2^n$. Now let us see what happens if the gunner has chosen another method and his enemy has discovered it through spies or sagacity. The method will in any case result in a series of shots and this series will be the same in two experiments if the series of signals 'before'

57

and 'beyond' is the same in both, because no other information is available for the gunner. Let us consider first $n = 1$, that is to say a single shot. There is no method possible to reduce the error beneath $L/2$ by a single shot. Only one method can reduce it to $L/2$ in all cases: shooting at the midpoint. If this method is adopted, there is no better method to reduce the distance by a subsequent shot than the method of hitting the midpoint of the first or of the second half, conforming to the signals 'beyond' or 'before'; this reduces the error to at most $L/4$. If, however, the first shot was not a shot at the center, there is for the enemy— who knew it before the battle—a segment greater than $L/2$ in which to place his tank. We know already that this distance can be halved by the gunner in the next shot if he has the best method, but even in this case it will give more than $L/4$ for the maximum error. Thus we have proved that the popular method of halving is best for $n = 2$. The same result follows for every n by induction. The classical method appears to be the best in the sense of the theory of games. We have not proved, however, that it is best in the sense of the theory of probability, i.e. that it reduces the expected distance to a minimum. Supposing all positions of the tank to be equally probable, we obtain the same solution as before.

The ranking of weights is quite a different problem from that treated already, if we are allowed to put several of them at once on the scale. If we have nine coins of the same appearance and we know that one of them is false and weighs less than any of the eight true coins, we can find the false one by two weighings. We put three coins on each side of the scale and if one side rises, we compare two of the three coins: if they are equal, the remaining third is false; if one of them is lighter, it is the false one. If, however, the first weighing gives no difference of weights, we compare two of the three remaining coins to discover the false one. The problem is more complicated if we have thirteen coins, one of which differs in weight from the others, but we don't know whether it is heavier or lighter than the standard coins. Nevertheless, three weighings are sufficient to find the forged coin (**61**). The coins are marked by numbers 1–13. The first column of the drawing shows the first weighing; there are eight coins involved, four on each arm, and two cases are possible: difference of weight or equality of weight. In every case a second weighing follows, which is to be seen in the second column, and in every case the second weighing leads to three possible results: (i) the arm with three coins 1, 2, 3 of the first set sinks; (ii) it rises; (iii) remains in balance. We have now six results possible and each of them leads to a weighing of a pair of coins. The results are to be seen in the third column: there are 18 items in the third column and the false piece is shown in a double circle; the arrow indicates whether it is heavier or lighter. In a single case we find the forged coin 13, without learning whether it is heavier or lighter than the true coins. To understand the procedure let us study the first line of the diagram. The first weighing has shown a difference between the coins 1, 2, 3, 4 and 5, 6, 7, 8. The false coin is among them. In the second weighing the coin 4 on the left arm has been replaced by 8; nevertheless the left arm went down as in the first weighing:—which proves that 4 and 8 are equal and thus sound. Now the first weighing has already shown that 9, 10, 11, 12, 13 are good coins; thus all coins on the right arm in

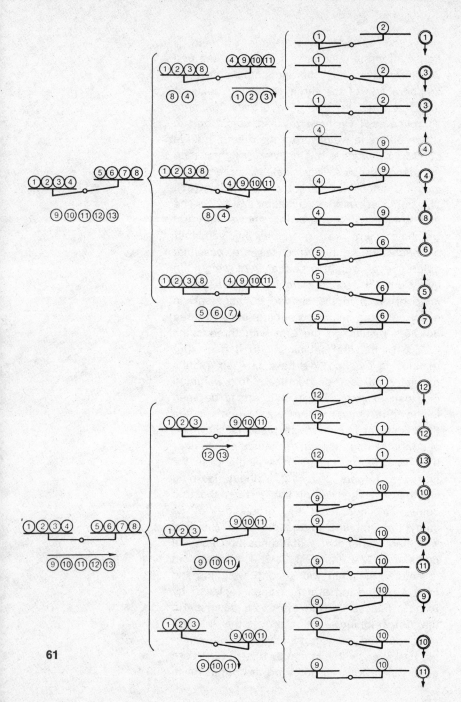

the second weighing are good, and, as there is inequality, it must be attributed to the left arm bearing 1, 2, 3, 8; as 8 is sound, one of the coins 1, 2, 3 is bad and too heavy. In the third step we compare 1 with 2 and see the arm with 1 going down,—which proves 1 to be bad and too heavy. In the same manner we get the results in all 18 cases. It is, however, interesting to study the case leading to the forged coin without saying whether it is too heavy or too light. The first weighing gives a balance between 1, 2, 3, 4 and 5, 6, 7, 8. The false coin is among 9, 10, 11, 12, 13; the horizontal arrow shows that we do not know if it is too heavy or too light. A second weighing shows equality of 1, 2, 3 and 9, 10, 11; these coins are sound, thus 12 or 13 is false. Comparing 12 with the sound 1, we get a balance in the third weighing, which proves 12 to be good and 13 to be bad; as 13 was not touched during the procedure, we do not know whether it is too light or too heavy.

It has been proved that n weighings are sufficient to find a bad coin among $(3^n - 1)/2$ coins and that this number cannot be diminished. The meaning of this assertion has been explained already: although no method of guaranteeing less than n weighing exists, we can find by accident the false coin among 13 in two weighings. Four weighings are sufficient and necessary for 40 coins. The reader may find a false coin among four by two weighings (the case $n = 2$).

Liquids are measured by vessels having a definite volume. If we have three vessels of respective volumes 12, 7, and 5 gallons and we have to divide 12 gallons of wine contained in the biggest vessel into equal parts, we can do it by using an appropriate billiard table (**62**) of rhomboid shape, the angles being 60°

61

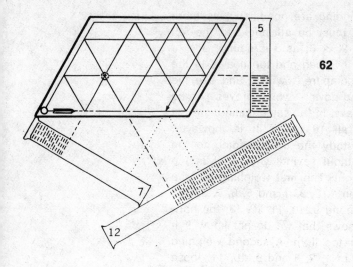

and 120°. We have to imagine the vessels lying on the plane of the table and the lines drawn from the billiard ball determining at every moment the levels of wine in the vessels.

Thus we divide the wine into two equal parts in the following way: we place the billiard ball in the lower left corner and direct it along the lower edge. As long as the billiard ball is rolling straight on, the wine is flowing, as shown in the figure (**62**), from the largest vessel into the medium one till the medium one is full; as the ball hits the edge and changes its direction in accordance with the laws of mechanics, the level of wine in the largest vessel remains unchanged, but it increases in the smallest one at the cost of the medium vessel, etc. This procedure continues until all the wine is divided into two equal parts. The figure (**62**) shows the broken path of the billiard ball; the end arrow marks the place where the portioning is accomplished.

This path consists of 11 straight portions—thus 11 acts are sufficient; this is the simplest solution. When driving the ball initially along the short side of the billiard table, we get another solution. (How many steps?)

If we have a rectangular billiard table, the ratio of whose sides (**63**) can be expressed by whole numbers (e.g. 5:3), a ball hit from a corner at an angle of 45° will strike one of the corners after several rebounds (in this case six). The explanation is supplied by the illustration (**64**), in which the broken course of the ball is replaced by a straight line. The rectangles represent the successive reflections of the billiard table in the edges (as in mirrors). If p:q is the ratio of the sides expressed in least integers, the ball rebounds $p + q - 2$ times before reaching the corner. (Why?)

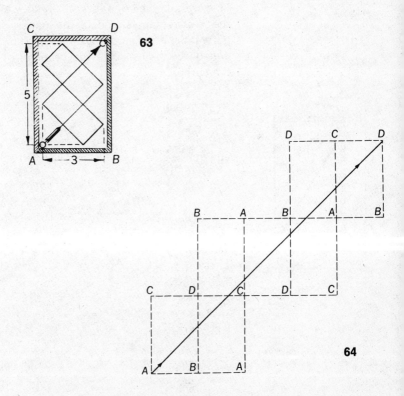

63

64

If we wish to hit ball B with ball A so that ball A will strike in succession the right, the lower, the left, and the upper edges, we must (**65**) find the reflected image B_1 of point B in the upper side, as in a mirror, then the reflected image B_2 of point B_1 in the left edge, then the image B_3 of point B_2 in the lower, and the image B_4 of point B_3 in the right edge. Then we aim at B_4 with ball A. We can ascertain every possible method of hitting our mark by forming a rectangular lattice, as in sketch (**64**), and placing in every rectangle the images B_1, B_2, B_3 ... of point B. By joining A to one of these B_n, we obtain a straight line; to get the broken course we have only to fold the rectangles along the common edges, beginning with the last one; eventually they all cover the first rectangle and, if the paper is transparent, the broken course appears. This method can be verified also in the problem of hitting the corner.

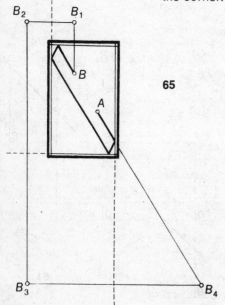

65

To divide an object like a cake into two equal parts, we can adopt the old custom of letting one partner cut and the other choose. The advantage of such a procedure is obvious: neither of the partners can object to this division. The first can secure the part due him by dividing the cake into two parts that he considers to be equally valuable; the second can secure at least his due part, by choosing the more valuable part or—if he considers them equally valuable—either part. It is presumed here that the object has the property of not losing its total value by division, i.e. that the values of the parts give by addition the value of the whole, this property being admitted by both partners, even if they disagree as to the valuation of the whole object and of its parts. There exist such objects: heaps of nuts, for instance. There arises the question of how to divide fairly an object into three or more parts. The answer is given by the following rules, which may be explained here in the case of five partners, the procedure being essentially the same for any number of partners. They may be called A, B, C, D, and E. A has the right to cut from the cake an arbitrary slice; B is free to diminish the slice cut off by A, but is not compelled to do so; in turn C has the right (but not the duty) to diminish the (already diminished or not diminished) slice, and so on. After E has made use of his right (or declined to do so), we see who was the last to touch the slice. Suppose it was D. Then D gets the slice, and the remainder of the cake (including the bits cut off) has to be divided fairly between A, B, C, and E. In the second round the same procedure reduces the number of partners to three, and the third round reduces it to two; the two partners divide the rest of the cake by the procedure initially explained: one cuts and the other chooses. Now let us see how every partner can secure his due part whatever his companions may do. If in the first round A cuts a slice that he considers to be 1/5 in value, it can happen that nobody touches it and A gets it; in this case he is not wronged. If, however, one or more of his companions diminish this slice, the man who was the last to touch it gets it and, as it is diminished, A must consider that more than 4/5 of the value is left to be divided equally among 4 partners, himself being one of them. In the second round A has to proceed as before: If he happens to be the first again, he has to cut a slice that he considers 1/4 in value of the remainder. This policy is not sufficient; we must show how a partner has to behave when he is not the first. Suppose that B considers the part cut by A to be too great, that is to say, greater in value in B's estimation than 1/5 of the whole. He has only to diminish it to the proper size; if he turns out to be the last diminisher, he gets it and is not wronged. If he fails to get it, it is because somebody else has touched the slice after it had already been diminished by B to a size considered by B as 1/5. One of these subsequent diminishers thus gets a slice that B considers to be of smaller value than 1/5, so that B comes to the next round as a shareholder of a remainder that he considers of greater value than 4/5 of the whole cake, the number of partners being now 4 and B one of them. Now the method is clear: if you are the first of n partners in any round, you have to cut off a slice that you consider to be $1/n$th in value of the part before you, whether it be the whole or the remainder of the cake; if you are not the first in the given round and you see a slice cut by one of your companions, a slice greater, in your estimation, than $1/n$th of the part, you have to diminish it to $1/n$th; if it has been cut so that the slice is $1/n$th or less, in your estimation, you have to keep off. This method insures that everybody receives what he considers to be his due share.

The 'fair division' gives the following game. A heap of different coins (**66**) is on a table inside a boundary, and the partners who have contributed equally to the heap have to divide it among themselves after the manner of our 'division of the cake.' Instead of a knife they have a rake with which they draw the coins beyond the boundary or back to the heap, a procedure corresponding to the 'cutting off' and 'diminishing' of the slices. As the actions have to be accomplished by one movement of the rake, the result depends on the discernment and skill of the players.

66

There is another problem of division encountered in economic life: the division of indivisible objects like houses, domestic animals, pieces of furniture, cars, and works of art. If, for instance, an inheritance composed of a house, a mill, and a car has to be divided among four inheritors A, B, C, D participating in equal shares, this division is generally made by a sworn appraiser who determines the values of the objects so that the inheritors can choose the objects and, if they agree, in principle, satisfy by payments in cash the mutual claims arising from the differences in value.

This procedure has many inconveniences connected with the determination of the objective value of things by an official appraiser or by a court of justice. It is possible to make a fair division without appealing to them:

An umpire, who has to act only as a sort of automaton to keep records and make computations, summons the inheritors to write down their estimates of the objects. They are not supposed to discuss the matter among themselves but every one of them is allowed to be helped by friends and experienced persons. Thus a table of values is put down by the umpire:

	A	B	C	D
House	$ 6,000	$ 10,000	$ 7,000	$ 9,000
Mill	3,000	2,000	4,000	2,000
Car	1,500	1,200	1,000	1,000
Sum	10,500	13,200	12,000	12,000
Share	2,625	3,300	3,000	3,000
Value	1,500	10,000	4,000	0
Claim	1,125	−6,700	−1,000	3,000

In the above table each person's share is got by dividing his estimate of the total by 4. In every row the greatest item appears in a frame and the corresponding object is attributed to the person whose name stands above the column. Thus A gets the car, B the house, and

C the mill. The values of the objects subtracted from the shares of the persons invested with them give the claims. *A* appears with a claim of $1,125, *D* with one of $3,000, whereas *B* has a negative claim of $6,700, and *C* a negative claim of $1,000. This means that *B* and *C* have to pay money to the umpire and *A* and *D* have to get money from him:

A	$1,125	B	$6,700	$7,700
D	3,000	C	1,000	−4,125
	4,125		7,700	3,575 ÷ 4 = $893.75

This computation shows that the payments will leave the umpire with a surplus of $3,575; divided by 4 this gives $893.75 for each inheritor. Thus

A will get the car and

$$1,125 + \$893.75 = \$2,018.75 \text{ cash}$$

B will get the house and will have to pay

$$\$6,700 - \$893.75 = \$5,806.25 \text{ off,}$$

C will get the mill and will have to pay

$$\$1,000 - \$893.75 = \$106.25 \text{ off,}$$

D will get $3,000 + $893.75 = $3,893.75.

Thus everybody will finally get more than his due share of the inheritance, the value of the total and of the objects given to him being estimated according to his own valuation. For instance, *A* has a car and $2,018.75 in cash; as the car is worth $1,500 to him, he has a total of $3,518.75, whereas he had estimated his share at only $2,625. He has got $893.75 over his due part and the same is true of other partners. This method works with unequal shares too, and it can be modified so as to diminish the payments in cash. (How?)

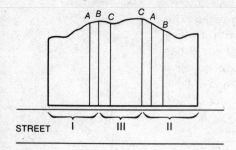

STREET I III II

67

The simplest way of dividing a plot of land is to do it on a map. Suppose that there are three joint proprietors of a garden wanting to divide it into three equal parts: they draw a sketch of the garden on transparent paper in 3 copies. Now every partner draws on his sketch two lines perpendicular to the street which, according to him, divide the garden into three equal parts. The parts do not need to be of equal area because the soil differs in quality and value, and besides, a man whose house is situated close to the garden estimates the soil near the house at a higher rate than the soil farther away—evidently the point in question is the subjective value. By superposing the transparent sketches one over the other we see six straight lines, which have been signed with the initials of the given names (Allan, Bertrand, Cecil). If the lines appear as shown in the above sketch (**67**), the umpire grants part I to *A*, part II to *B* and part III to *C*, thus giving to each partner more than 1/3 of the garden (in value) in the partners' own estimation. There are 8 different possibilities but there is always a division possible which gives to each person at least as much as his own estimation of 1/3 of the lot. The advantage of this method (dividing on a map) is that all shareholders are admitted simultaneously to the determination of parts; the provisional dividing lines remain unknown to those partners who did not draw them. The role of the umpire is purely automatic, and is settled by the principle that each partner has to get at least as much as his estimation of a third of the garden. In some of the 8 different cases the umpire bisects some strips without, however, violating the principle.

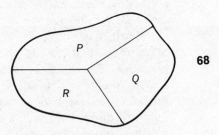

The fair division of a cake into three parts can be achieved as follows:

Partner *A* draws three lines (**68**) on the cake; he has to declare that the three parts *P, Q, R* defined by these lines are for him of equal value. It could happen that *B* considers *P* as good for him; he will be given *P* for the asking. If *C* likes *Q*, he can acquire it; then *A* takes *R*: his declaration implies his satisfaction without being asked. Our supposition, however, is too optimistic: it could happen that *B* and *C* both consider *R* as good, that is, of value above one-third of the cake's value, and they declare *P* and *Q* as bad, i.e. each of these parts beneath one-third of the cake's value. Then *A* takes *P*; as *B* and *C* give to *P* a value beneath one-third of the cake they must admit that the part *Q + R* has a value above two-thirds of the cake's value; it follows that *B* and *C* can divide the part *Q + R* after the principle 'one divides, the other chooses.'

There is the problem of division of seats in proportional polling. We shall explain it for three parties, A, B, and C, assuming that the proportion of votes registered is exactly reckoned and the seats in the Assembly proportionately distributed. To avoid fractions each party is first allowed as many seats as are indicated by the integral numbers; then the fractions are arranged according to their magnitude and each party receives a supplementary seat for its fraction in turn till all seats are distributed. For example, a district returns 5 members and counts 150,000 voters. The parties A, B, C gathered 43,500, 69,000, and 37,500 votes respectively. Hence their claims are 1.45, 2.3, and 1.25 seats respectively. First they are given 1, 2, and 1 seats respectively and the remainders 0.45, 0.3, and 0.25 indicate that the fifth seat must fall to party A. The result of the election is therefore: A—2 seats, B—2 seats, C—1 seat. If we have an equilateral triangle (**69**) with a height of 5 units, the sum of the distances of any given point in its interior from the three sides A, B, C will always be 5 units. As there are 150,000 voters and 5 seats, we can represent a seat or 30,000 votes by one unit. By this convention every polling will be represented by a point in the triangle, the distances from the sides, A, B, C measured in units giving the number of seats won theoretically by the parties A, B, C. For instance, the point indicated by the spot corresponds to the result of the election as mentioned above, for its distances from the sides A, B, C are 1.45, 2.3, and 1.25 units respectively. All those points that lead in practice to the same distribution of seats fill a regular hexagon; in our example this hexagon is indicated by 2, 2, 1. The distribution of seats being written in each hexagon, we may, by reckoning up the number of votes,

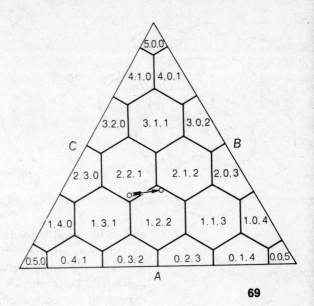

69

obtain the final result of the election directly from the sketch, without computing the remainders. The arrow on the sketch shows how it can happen that, with the total number of votes unchanged, party A can in the next election gain votes and lose a seat; this seat can be gained only by another party that has increased its votes. (Does this agree with what happens in the case designated by the reverse arrow?)

The system of distribution of seats as shown here is called the 'system of least remainders.' There are several other systems of proportional representation but none of them escapes the paradox of a party's gaining votes and losing a seat: Every polling system leads to a division of an equilateral triangle into regions. Three regions (**70**), corresponding to the triples (2,2,1), (2,1,2) and (1,2,2) border with one another. Trying to avoid the paradox mentioned

73

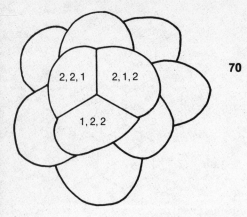

70

above, we must draw two lines that will form the frontiers of the region (1,2,2) in such a way that the angle between them, measured inside (1,2,2), is greater than 180°. The same must hold for both regions. However, not all of these angles can be greater than 180°, because they add to 360°.

4

Tessellations, Mixing of Liquids, Measuring Areas and Lengths

Our sketch of proportional elections reminds us of a honeycomb. The photograph (**71**) shows the plane filled up by hexagonal cells. No more than three hexagons meet in a point; this is the only case in which every vertex is 'of degree three' (**72**); every other division exhibits points where more than three regions meet.

The tessellation with squares has already been shown (**15**). By distortion we can derive from it a tessellation with arbitrary quadrilaterals (**73**). The tessellation with triangles (**74**) is the last of this class; if we are restricted to only one shape and size of tile, this tile being a regular polygon, no other tessellation is possible.

71

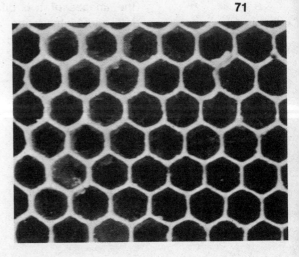

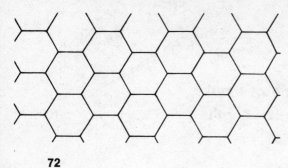

72

73

After an easy training one develops the faculty of seeing the lattice (**74**) raised a few inches above the page—the reason for this phenomenon is the possibility of conceiving the images of two different triangles on the left and right retina as resulting from one triangle placed above the page. The training

74

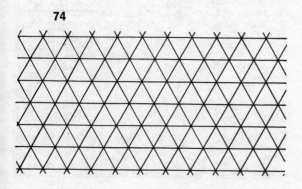

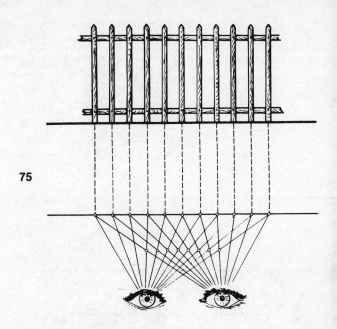

75

consists in learning to look crosswise, as explained by sketch (**75**), at two triangles and the principal difficulty is in accommodating the lenses to the distance of the page when the axes of the eyes are both aimed at a point above the page.

The whole plane can also be covered with convex heptagons (**76**).

76

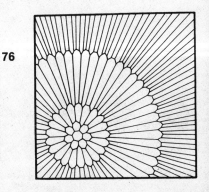

By using simultaneously various regular polygons to fill up the plane, each vertex being a common point of the same number of polygons of the same shape as those meeting in any other vertex, we obtain a homogeneous tessellation. As the angle of a regular n-gon equals $2 - 4/n$ right angles or $1/2 - 1/n$ of a complete angle, to determine the tessellation we must find positive integers $n, p, q, r \ldots$ such as will give

$$1/2 - 1/n + 1/2 - 1/p + 1/2$$
$$- 1/q + \ldots = 1.$$

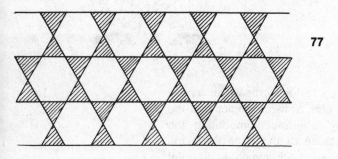

77

78

This way leads to 17 different patterns, but only 11 of these can be extended over the whole plane without overlapping. These are the three tessellations already mentioned and the eight following: (77), (78), (79), (80), (81), (82), (83), (84). Non-homogeneous tessellations are perhaps even more beautiful: (85), (86), (87), (88), (89); their number is unlimited. (Why?)

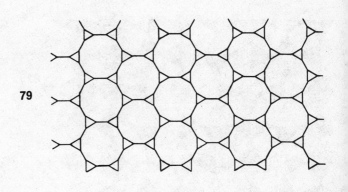

79

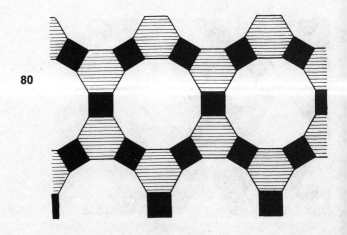

80

81

82

83

84

85

86

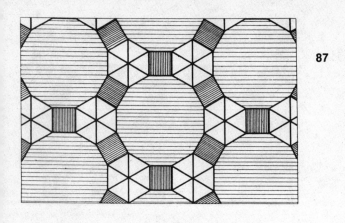

87

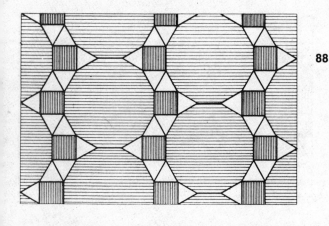

88

89

Which tessellation is the best? The first one (**72**), i.e. the hexagonal one to be seen on a honeycomb. 'Best' means that in such a division of the whole plane into regions of one acre each, the amount of material required for fences shall be as small as possible; this happens when the regions have the form of regular hexagons.

We can apply the division of the plane to the manufacture of shoes. Human feet have different sizes; putting on the corner of a board a rectangle with the same breadth and length as the foot, the opposite corner of the rectangle fixes a point on the board. There are as many points as there are different feet. A factory wanting to produce men's shoes should with the help of shoe shops obtain the measurements of several men's feet and these measurements will give a set of points on the measuring board, which forms a fairly coherent region, i.e. only a few points lie far away from the rest. For those few abnormal feet, the factory will not produce shoes. On the other hand practice shows that for normal men's feet, 27 types of different lengths and breadths are sufficient. If the factory intends to produce 27 different types of shoes, the question arises as to the choice of the sizes. Obviously, for that purpose we must choose 27 points on the measuring board in such a way that each point of the plane is as near as possible to one of the 27 points.

The points are distributed as on sketch (**40**); this is the routine method. Every point can be regarded as the middle of a square and the routine solution leads consequently to the square pattern. Our statement, however, suggests a hexagonal pattern, where each point is the middle of a regular hexagon (**90**). For our purpose the second tessellation is a better

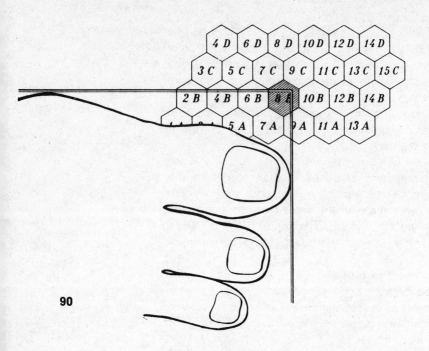

90

one: the number of types remaining the same, the distance of the chosen point from the neighboring points is about 7 per cent less; this improves the fitting of shoes.

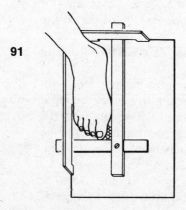

91

Suppose we have a measuring board with a hexagonal tessellation (**91**); on each field the type of shoe is marked. To find the correct type of shoes the foot must be placed in the corner of the measuring board, which has been provided with a raised rim. On the foot one must place a movable marker; from the hexagon thus indicated we read off the correct size of shoes.

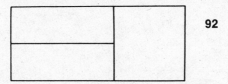

92

Flying above our country, one sees the whole land divided into rectangular lots, some of them very small. This is the effect of division of inheritances among successors. Assuming that such divisions never employ shapes other than rectangular ones, one sees immediately that a figure like (**92**) is ambiguous: it could be the effect of the division among three sons or, as well, between two sons, one of whom has divided his lot in turn among his two successors. It has been proved that a rectangle composed of 3 or 4 or 6 rectangular lots is always ambiguous. We call primitive a figure which is unambiguous: the following figures are all primitive (**93**).

93

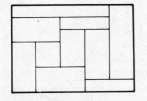 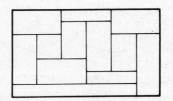 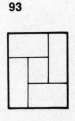

It is possible to build primitive patterns of very great numbers of lots (**94**). They are obviously better for a pattern of bricks in a wall than the ambiguous ones. The reader may find further numbers of lots which can be encountered in primitive patterns.

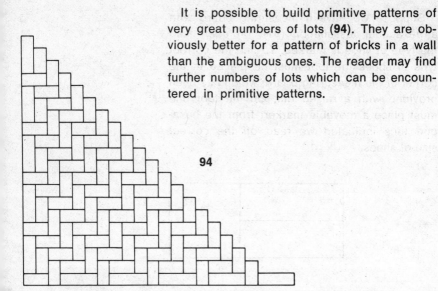

94

Sketch (**95**) shows a standard pattern of a wall: the bricks are arranged in horizontal layers; an earthquake could shift the upper layers horizontally along the lower ones. The wall (**96**) has not this drawback: no horizontal

95

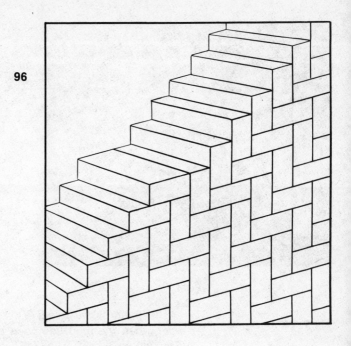

96

sliding is possible; even more: no plane section
whatever could divide the construction without
cutting some bricks. The wall **(97)** is more
sophisticated but no better than **(96)**.

97

98

The patterns we observe on the shore of a river when the mud has been dried up by the sun (**98**) or in an earthenware jar held empty against the sunlight (**99**) seem to be quite irregular; nevertheless as a rule they show right angles. This can be explained by assuming the cracking to be an effect of contraction; the line appearing as a fissure has, by a principle of mechanics, to make the work of disjunction as small as possible. The work is proportional to the areas of the sections and the lines must have a course such as to minimize the surfaces laid open by the fissure. This procedure gives right angles if the clay is homogeneous; the varying thickness of the layer accounts for the curvature of the lines. This remark supplies in many cases a means of deciding which line appeared earlier and which later: the older of the two splits passes right through the point of junction. Thus we can follow the genealogy of splits and eventually find the ancestors of the whole system.

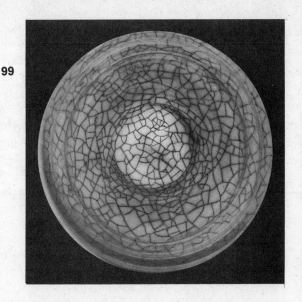

99

Suppose the pattern was composed initially of two regions, *A* and *B*. A new line appears, joining two points of two already existing arcs and giving rise to a new region *C* (**100**); since the new line breaks up two arcs into two parts each, the number of arcs increases by three. After n steps we have n more regions and $3n$ more arcs. Since there were initially two regions and three arcs, we now have $n + 2$ regions and $3n + 3$ arcs.

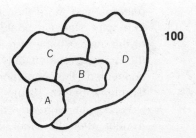

100

Let us apply this idea to maps. If we consider the exterior (the ocean) as a region too, we have $n + 3$ regions and $3n + 3$ frontiers. Every frontier is common to two regions and, by drawing it, we increase the number of 'neighborships' by two: X-Y and Y-X. Thus we eventually have $6n + 6$ 'neighborships,' and the average number of neighbors to a country is $(6n + 6)/(n + 3) = 6 - 12/(n + 3)$. For an isle divided into k states the average number of neighbors to a state is $6 - 12/(k + 1)$. This number is less than 6, but tends to 6, as the number of countries increases. Now we must remember that the ocean counts as a country and that the number k of dry countries is equal to $n + 2$, so that the average number of neighborships is $6 - 12/(k + 1)$.

Now we want to disregard the ocean and the coastline as a frontier. In this way we lose one country and at least 6 neighborships, the number of coastlands being at least 3. As the average number of neighborships is less than 6, the mean value diminishes and will be less than $6 - 12/(k + 1)$ and in consequence, less than 6.

We have assumed that the number of coastlands was at least 3. But we may draw a map consisting of, say 10 countries, which will contain only one or two coastlands. This will occur only if we allow annular countries, or those having several disconnected frontiers in common. We have not taken into consideration patterns with more than three regions meeting in a point. Now we would like to see if the rule of the impossibility of reaching 6 applies to all the maps, provided only that the regions are connected (this condition was not fulfilled in Germany, before 1870).

We begin with any region and draw one frontier after the other, each time connecting two frontier points. It may happen that such a line does not create a new region (when?), but then it will not form any new neighborship either. If it does create a new region then it will be only one, while the number of arcs may increase by 1, 2, or 3. They yield at most 6 new neighborships and thus our reasoning holds: the average number of neighborships is less than 6. But now we have still to get rid of the ocean which in our computation counts as a region. Nevertheless, the rule applies on any map drawn, if we count only the mainland for regions and land frontiers for frontiers. This may be verified by inspecting different patterns, but the proof seems to be rather deep. The author is not even certain that such a proof exists.

Let us imagine that from the first year on we observe the growth of a child in the following way: on a white ledge we mark with a black dash the child's height and write the child's age opposite the dash. 1 denotes the end of the first year, 1.1—the end of 1/10 of the second year, 2—the end of the second year, etc.

Suppose the rate of growth to be inversely proportional to time; i.e. the increase of a child of two years is half as great as for a one-year-old; the increase of a child of three, compared to that of a one-year-old, is one-third as great, etc. Then the numbers on the ledge form a scale, which has been called logarithmic. Such scales are to be found on the so-called 'logarithmic slide rule,' two above and two below; of these four scales the two central ones are engraved upon a sliding rule (**101**). No matter what the position of the rule may be (**102**), the numbers standing immediately above each other are proportional. Here, for instance, the numbers on the fixed upper scale are 2.45

101

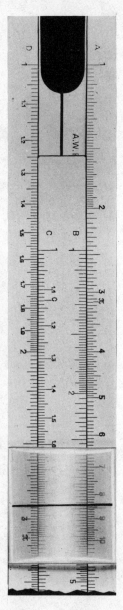

102

times greater than those on the margin immediately beneath them, so that if, for example, we wish to multiply 3.45 by 2.45, we move the window with the hair to 3.45 on the slide, then read off above 8.45 as the product. On the lower scales we see 1.565, 1.86, 2.91. The error amounts to about 0.3 per cent. The numbers on the uppermost scale are squares of the numbers standing beneath them on the lowest scale. The hair indicator in the photograph shows $2.91^2 = 8.45$. It is therefore possible to extract the square root by means of the slide rule. (How?) The slide rule is especially useful in solving rule-of-three problems.

When mixing two liquids of different specific gravities, e.g. two kinds of gasoline, we can use the nomogram (**103**) to determine the specific gravity of the mixture. The broad oblique scale on the sketch is movable; at the point where it intersects the left-hand vertical line we read the specific gravity of the lighter liquid; at the point where it cuts the right-hand vertical line, we get the specific gravity of the heavier liquid, while the fixed oblique scale shows in the intersection with the movable one the specific gravity of the mixture on the movable scale and the percentage of the heavier liquid on itself. To compute the specific gravity of a mixture composed of 55 per cent oil with specific gravity .830, and 45 per cent gasoline with specific gravity .543, we lay down the movable scale with the points .830 and .543 on the vertical lines and shift it vertically until it crosses the point 55 on the fixed scale; in this very point we read from the movable scale .701, which is the specific gravity of the mixture we had to find out. The theorem follows from the similarity of triangles formed by the scales. The two oblique, heavy lines must be used if the specific gravities of the components

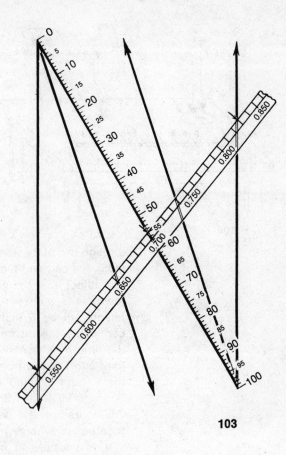

103

have a difference less than 20 per cent; their role is the same as that of the verticals. Knowing any three of the data we can find the fourth; for instance, the specific gravities of both components and that of the mixture being given, the nomogram yields easily the percentage of the components. (How?)

There are simpler nomograms known. Such is the nomogram of the lens. The distance f, g, h of the object, the image, and the focus from the lens (**104**) are connected according to an optical law by the formula $1/f + 1/g = 1/h$. Therefore, by drawing a straight line

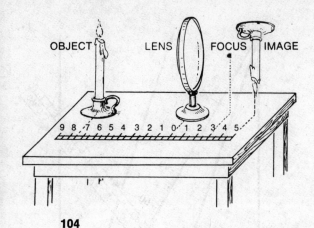

OBJECT   LENS   FOCUS   IMAGE

9 8 7 6 5 4 3 2 1 0 1 2 3 4 5

104

through two of these numbers on the nomogram (**105**), we can find the third. Here, for instance, the object is at the distance of 7.5 inches, the focus is 3 inches from the lens, hence the image will be 5 inches behind the lens. We can apply this nomogram to the question of the time *h* necessary to accomplish a task by joint effort of two men, who would need separately *f* and *g* hours for it. (If a man needs 5 hours to fill a car with coal and his apprentice 7.5 hours for the same job, they will do it together in 3 hours.)

It is possible to draw nomograms without providing them with scales of numbers. If we notice that the musical scale is a logarithmic one, i.e. similar to the scales on the slide rule (**101**), because the number of vibrations keeps

105

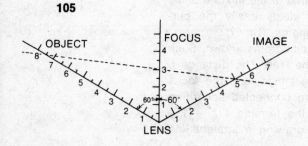

OBJECT   FOCUS   IMAGE

LENS

rising by a constant factor as we pass one tone higher, we can construct the following nomogram (**106**), which permits us to read the radius of one meter of wire weighted by 100 kilograms, provided the material and the pitch are given. For example, the dotted line on the column indicates the radius of an iron wire tuned to 'A.' Inversely, material and radius being given, we may also ascertain the pitch of the note. The construction is based on Mersenne's formula

$$n = \frac{1}{2Lr} \sqrt{\frac{P}{d\pi}}$$

(*n* number of vibrations per second, *L* length in meters, *P* stretching force in kilograms, *r* radius of the section in millimeters, *d* density of the material in grams per cubic centimeter, $\pi = 3.14159\ldots$). Some spaces between the music lines are greater than others. (Why?)

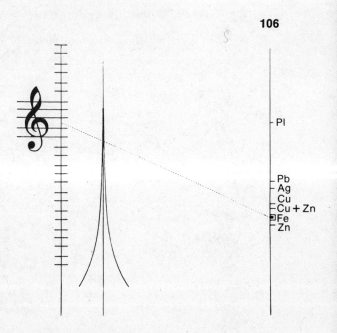

The polygon on the lattice of whole numbers (**107**) illustrates the following theorem: the area of any polygon whose vertices are points of the lattice is equal to the number of interior lattice points, plus half the number of lattice points on the border, minus 1. For instance, in the present case the area is

$$6 + \frac{11}{2} - 1 = 10.5.$$

We can verify it easily for a rectangle. If its base is m units and its height n units, its area is mn units. On the border there are 4 vertices $2(m - 1)$ points on both bases, and $2(n - 1)$ points on both vertical sides: together there are $b = 2m + 2n$ border points. The interior points form $m - 1$ columns and $n - 1$ rows; there are $i = (m - 1)(n - 1)$ interior points. The rule gives for the area A the number $i + b/2 - 1$ equal to

$$(m - 1)(n - 1) + (2m + 2n)/2 - 1 = mn,$$

which is the true value. The next step is the

107

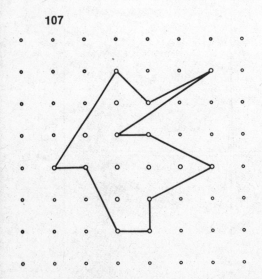

observation that two polygons with a common side can be combined into one polygon by suppressing that side, and that the number $i + b/2 - 1$ for the new polygon equals the sum of the analogous numbers corresponding to the component polygons. It follows that the number $i + b/2 - 1$ corresponding to a triangle resulting from halving a rectangle by its diagonal is one half of the number corresponding to the rectangle and therefore equal to the area of the triangle. Now we can get every polygon by adding and subtracting appropriate triangles and finally we get the rule

$$A = i + b/2 - 1$$

for every polygon with vertices on the lattice.

To measure areas we can utilize the lattice of whole numbers even for arbitrary domains. We can always shift a domain to such a position that the number of lattice points covered by the domain equals or surpasses the area of the domain. For example (**108**) the shaded area has 11 units. Let us place it as we please

108

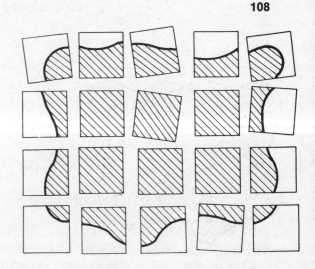

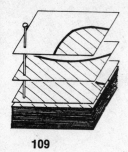

109

on the lattice and cut along the lines of the lattice. The whole figure breaks up into squares; placing them one upon another (**109**), we shall be able to pierce the pile with a pin so as to strike the shaded parts at least 11 times. To explain this, let us suppose that we can strike the shaded parts 10 times at most; then the basic square would be covered at most 10 times by the shaded parts and the whole domain would have an area at most equal to 10 units, contrary to our knowledge. Having discovered a point with the required property, we spread the squares beside one another again (**110**) and we see 11 (or more) pin pricks in the domain; then we move the domain, shifting it in such a way that one pin prick covers a lattice-point; then all of them will. Our argument is valid also for a domain with an area of 10.1 units. (Why?)

If no great exactness is required, we can utilize a lattice to measure areas. For instance, to measure the area of a leaf, we cover it with a celluloid film dotted as shown in (**107**), the distances apart being 3.16 millimeters. We count the points covered by the leaf; if there

110

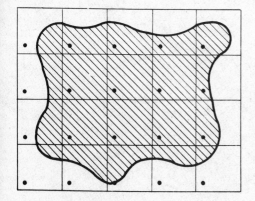

are *n* of them, the area of the leaf approximately amounts to 10*n* square millimeters. This method can be improved by distributing the points as shown in the sketch (**111**). By what distance should they be separated?

Let us take a convex closed curve of an area 4, having a center, i.e. a point that halves all chords through it. Now let us place this domain on the lattice of integers (**112**) in such a way that the center becomes one of the points of the lattice; otherwise it is immaterial how it is placed. The domain will now enclose at least two more points of the lattice: this is one of Minkowski's discoveries in geometry.

112

We shall make use of this theorem (the proof of which is not obvious) to estimate how far we may see through an array of hop-poles. We are supposed to be looking from a point occupied previously by a hop-pole, which we have removed to place our eye exactly in a lattice point. The projections of the hop-poles are (**113**) little circles of radius r. The line of sight continues only until it comes nearer to a lattice point than r. Let us draw a straight line through our observation point, extending to the distance $1/r$ on both sides, and let us consider this segment as the median of a rectangle with $2r$ as base. The area of the

113

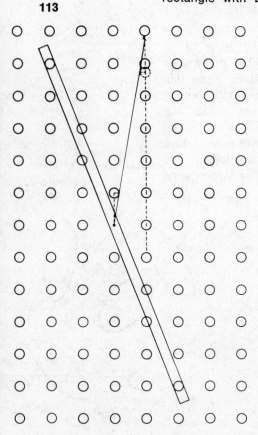

rectangle is 4 and its center is a lattice point; by Minkowski's theorem at least two lattice points more will fall on the rectangle or in its interior. The circles surrounding them will consequently touch or cut the median of the rectangular strip and cut off our sight. Thus we cannot see farther than $1/r$. But we can see almost as far. To prove it let us look in a direction touching the next circle in the same row. Let us prolong the line of sight to the next parallel row and let us compute at what distance it cuts the central (dashed) line of that row. It is easy to see that the large right triangle is similar to the small one; we have to compute the hypotenuse h of the large one: the similarity gives the proportion $h : 1 = 1 : r$ and consequently $h = 1/r$. But we cannot see as far as h, because in the next row there are circles interfering with our sight. Let us move such a circle along the central (dashed) line of the next row until it touches the line of sight. Thus we get another triangle, congruent to our small one. Its side along the line of sight is $\sqrt{1 - r^2}$ and this amount is to be subtracted from $1/r$ to get the range of sight in the worst case. Of course our line of sight already touches a small circle in the first row, but by slightly altering the angle we can avoid this obstacle, and our outlook is shortened only by a very small amount. Thus we can say that our sight can reach certain points whose distance is almost equal to $1/r - \sqrt{1 - r^2}$, but it cannot reach any point farther than $1/r$. For instance, when the poles have a diameter of 2 inches and are standing 20 inches apart, we have, taking 20 inches as our unit, $r = 0.05$; we get $1/r = 20$ units $= 400$ inches and $1/r - \sqrt{1 - r^2} = 19.0013$ units $= 380.026$ inches. Thus the farthest point visible has a distance between 380.026 and 400 inches.

The measuring of areas is easier than the measuring of lengths. This is so because if a contour is given with a certain accuracy, we can estimate the area enclosed by it with an error that becomes less and less as the accuracy increases and can be made as small as we like. It is quite a different matter with lengths. Two curved lines lying very near one another can differ considerably in their lengths: the zigzag line (**114**), for instance, is about 40 per cent longer than the straight one. There

114

are lines of infinite length, if we admit the existence of things defined correctly in mathematical language and do not care for real models. Mathematicians need such curves for theoretical purposes. Such a theoretical problem, for instance, is how to draw a curve passing through every point of a square, where we mean by 'square' all points of the interior and the boundary. Sierpiński solves the problem by beginning with a closed polygon (**115**), then uniting four similar polygons (**116**) into one cross, after which he joins four figures similar to the cross (**117**), and so on (**118**), repeating (**119**) the construction. The limit of these approximations is the curved line filling the square: We may regard it as the track of a moving point, and for every point in the square indicate the precise moment when the moving point will pass through that given point. The curve has an infinite length. It is impossible to draw it in its final perfect stage. (Why?)

Looking steadily at the sketch (**119**) we see oblique lines which tend to appear and disappear. (Why?)

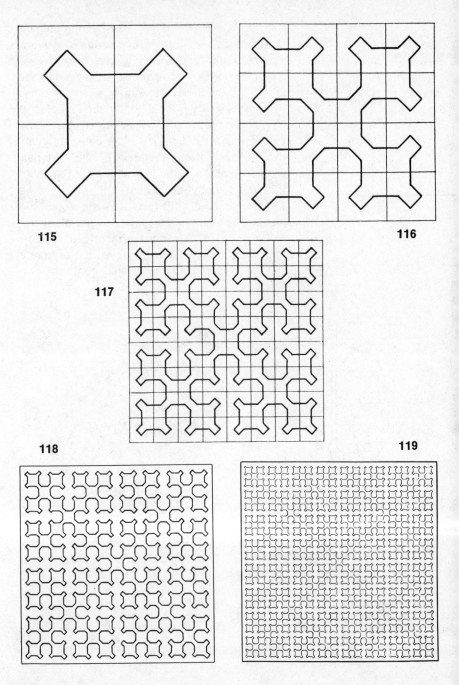

115

116

117

118

119

Given any closed curve, like Lake Michigan, for instance, we can circumscribe a square about it. This fact is easy to see, because we can (**120**) first circumscribe a rectangle by taking a pair of parallel tangents, and another parallel pair orthogonal to the first one, and then turn the whole frame round the fixed curve; after a rotation of 90° the pairs are interchanged and if the distance of the first pair was originally greater than that of the second, it became finally less. There must therefore be a moment when both distances are equal and just at that moment the tangents form a square.

We show (**121**) a square inscribed in Lake Michigan; it is difficult to prove that a square can be inscribed in any closed contour.

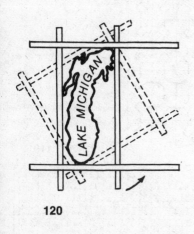

120

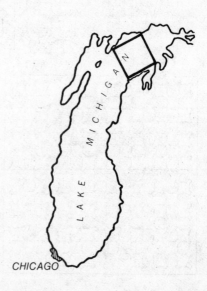

121

To measure lengths we can make use of a sort of chessboard. On a transparent sheet there is a lattice of straight lines forming squares with sides 3.82 mm. One family of lines is inclined 30° to the frame of the sheet. To measure the length of the Mississippi River, for instance, we put the frame of the sheet on the frame of the map (**122**) and travel along the river, from its source to the sea, as if the

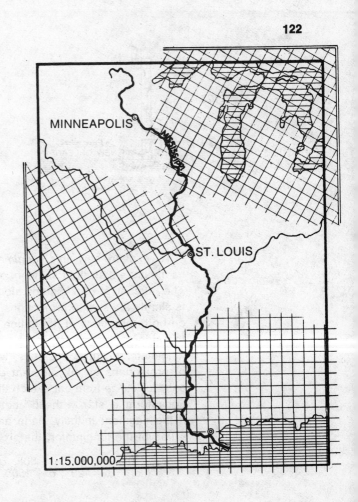

122

MINNEAPOLIS

MISSISSIPPI

ST. LOUIS

1:15,000,000

end of our pencil were a rook (**123**) wandering on a chessboard. Counting the steps, we then put the sheet with one of its lines on the frame of the map and do as before, finally proceeding as we did the first time but with the sheet reversed. The total number of steps gives the length in mm; as the map is 1: 15,000,000, we have to multiply the total by 15 to get the length of the Mississippi in kilometers (or by 9.321 to get it in miles).

123

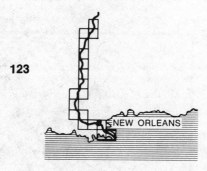

NEW ORLEANS

To explain how this *longimeter* works, let us measure a straight segment of L millimeters. The number of rook's steps along the segment is simply the sum of projections of the segment on both directions of the lattice, when we take the side of the squares as a unit. Putting the longimeter in three positions, we get the sum of projections on six different directions; it is easy to realize from our sketch that these directions form a star with 30° between its rays. If the segment initially made an angle α with a line of the longimeter, the six angles will be

$$\alpha + 0°, \; \alpha + 30°, \; \alpha + 60°, \; \alpha + 90°,$$
$$\alpha + 120°, \; \alpha + 150°.$$

The sum of the projections will be

$$L\{\sin(\alpha + 0°) + \sin(\alpha + 30°)$$
$$+ \sin(\alpha + 60°) + \sin(\alpha + 90°)$$
$$+ \sin(\alpha + 120°) + \sin(\alpha + 150°)\}.$$

We don't know α but we find that the expression above becomes least for $\alpha = 0°$ and greatest for $\alpha = 15°$. Thus the least value is

$$L(0 + 1/2 + \sqrt{3}/2 + 1 + \sqrt{3}/2 + 1/2) = 3.732L,$$

and the greatest value is

$$L\left(\frac{\sqrt{6} - \sqrt{2}}{4} + \frac{\sqrt{2}}{2} + \frac{\sqrt{6} + \sqrt{2}}{4}\right.$$
$$\left. + \frac{\sqrt{6} + \sqrt{2}}{4} + \frac{\sqrt{2}}{2} + \frac{\sqrt{6} - \sqrt{2}}{4}\right)$$
$$= 3.864L.$$

As our unit is 3.82, we have to divide the results by 3.82 to get the sums of projections in mm. We get now $0.977L$ and $1.011L$ instead of L. Thus we get the length of every segment with an error between -2.3 and 1.1 per cent. As we can consider every curve as composed of short straight segments, the relative error of its length as computed by the longimeter will not exceed these limits; in most cases it will be even smaller. (Why?)

On some maps contour lines are drawn to show the vertical configuration of the land. By measuring their total length, one can compute the average declivity of the district. This can be done with the aid of the longimeter by counting the number of intersections of the lattice with the lines.

To find the direction and magnitude of maximal slope of an inclined terrain (this has practical value, for instance, in drainage) we need no complicated measurements nor diffi-

107

cult computations: we simply measure the slope in any direction *OX* and mark off on the line *OX* on the map as many inches as the slope in percentage amounts to. This we repeat in the direction *OY*, which is perpendicular to *OX*. Now we complete the sketch to a rectangle, the diagonal of which gives us the direction and magnitude of the maximal slope. In example (**124**) the maximal slope is 5 per cent. A measuring tape, a measuring lath with a scale, and an aiming device with a water level are all we need.

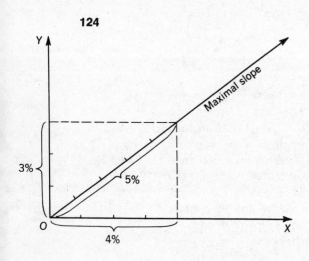

124

There still remains the question of the length of a line given by nature and not by a mathematical definition. When measuring the length of a river, one is faced with the problem of small sinuosities of its course. Some countries have as their frontiers tortuous rivers or mountain ridges. By employing more and more detailed maps and increasing the accuracy of measurement to a corresponding degree, we can get the length to be about as great as we like. The longimeter is a remedy for this inconvenience, but the drawback of the device is that its accuracy is limited by the size of the real square corresponding (for a given map) to the longimeter's square. This size may vary, and it would be difficult to give definite rules; such rules would prescribe different scales and appropriate longimeters for different purposes. There is, however, the method of measuring lengths by counting the number n of intersections of a set of parallel lines with the curve considered; if d is the distance of the lines and k the number of different positions of the set, then $L = nd\pi/2k$ is the approximate length. We have to turn the transparent sheet carrying the lines through an angle of $180°/k$ from one position to the next. To avoid the paradox of length noted above, we can agree to discard on every line its 11th and subsequent intersections with the curve. Thus we get what may be called L_{10}, the length of order 10. This concept is free from the paradox of length; if we employ more and more detailed maps and increase the accuracy of measurement by reducing d and increasing k, keeping the restriction to 10 intersections at most per line, the numbers L computed by the formula above will approach more and more closely a definite limit, the ideal value of L_{10}. In the same manner lengths of any order $L_1, L_2, \ldots, L_m, \ldots$ could be defined. This principle opens a way to rules of measuring that are free from such units as miles or yards: to compare the lengths of frontiers, the length of order 12, for instance, could be adopted for all countries.

Let us call L'_m the length of the left bank of the Mississippi, L''_m the length of the right bank, both of the mth order; we still have the paradox

$$\lim_{m \to \infty} L'_m = \infty; \lim_{m \to \infty} L''_m = \infty$$

Nevertheless, we can reasonably expect the limit of the ratio L'_m/L''_m to be finite. This limit can be measured to any desired accuracy: we have only to choose m sufficiently great and apply the method described above. Thus we could measure the ratio of the lengths of both banks without determining the true lengths themselves. We leave it to the reader to explain the meaning of L_2 for the boundary of a region.

5

Shortest Paths, Locating Schools, and Pursuing Ships

The straight line is the shortest path. An Arab wishes to return to his tent, but on the way he wants to feed his horse and draw water from a river. Which is he to do first? **(125)** The tent reflected in the river's bank gives a point a_1, while this point reflected in turn in the border of the pasture gives a_2. When the order of successive reflections is reversed, we obtain A_1 and A_2. The black, full, zigzag line is the shortest way; it is equal to the distance of point a_2 from the Arab's position. If he wished to water his horse first, the path would be at least as long as the distance in a straight line to A_2, which is more. The Arab did not draw any plan; he simply aimed his musket at the point where the pasture and river meet, and seeing that point lying on the left of his tent, rode off to the left. To explain his behavior let us remark first that the points a_2 and A_2 can be found without knowing the position of the Arab. All his possible positions can be classified as those nearer to a_2, those nearer to A_2, and those equally distant from a_2 and A_2. The last positions, called neutral points, form a straight line, the division line. For an Arab already in the tent, who wants to feed his horse, draw water from the river, and return to his tent, it is immaterial what he does first: any path from tent to pasture to river to tent has the same length as the same path back: tent — river —

pasture — tent. From this we conclude that, in the case when he starts at the tent, the order of succession is immaterial. The order obviously does not matter for a rider standing at the point where the river cuts the pasture. So we have *two* neutral points: the intersection point of pasture and river and the tent. The division line must pass through both. The Arab, seeing the intersection to the left of the tent, is himself to the left of the division line, and, consequently, nearer to a_2 than to A_2. As the

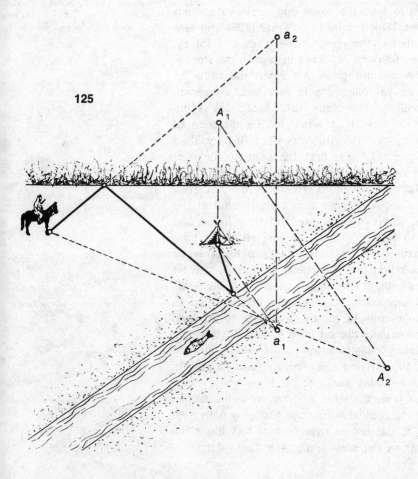

125

shortest paths are as long as his distances from a_2 and A_2, he chooses the itinerary drawn on our picture and equal to his distance from a_2. The principle of reflection employed here is the same as in our billiard problems.

To reach the village V from T a tourist paddles at a speed of 5 miles per hour to the shore and continues walking across the country at 4 miles per hour. To get to this village in the shortest time possible, he travels along the path shown on sketch (**126**).

Three villages are to build a common school. In order to reduce as far as possible the total time spent by pupils in traveling to school, they have to find an appropriate spot for the location of the school. They have, for instance, 50, 70, and 90 children respectively. Stretching

126

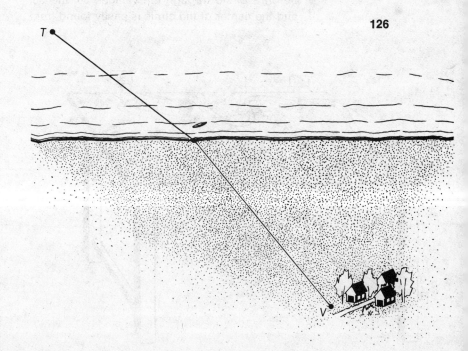

out the map of the district on a table (**127**), we make holes in the table where the villages are, pass three strings through the holes, tie the upper ends into a knot, and weight the lower ones with 50, 70, and 90 ounces respectively. The school should be built where the knot is caught. But ruining the table is not necessary. We first draw a triangle (**128**) with sides 50, 70, and 90 units (choosing any unit we like): we are interested in the external angles ⧣, ⧣, and ⧣, of this auxiliary triangle. Now we have to find on the map a point from which the villages are visible in directions that form the same angles. So, for instance, the villages 50 and 90 have to be seen (**129**) at the same angle as the external angle enclosed by the sides 50 and 90 of the auxiliary triangle. The points on the map responding to this condition lie on a circle through the villages 50 and 90, and the center of the circle is easily found from

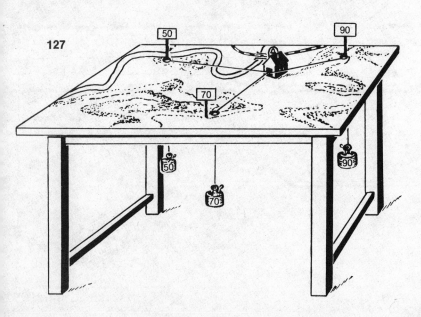

127

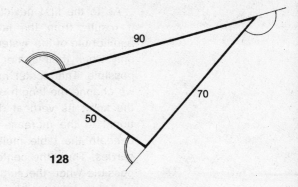

128

the proposition that the central angle corresponding to both villages equals twice the internal angle of the auxiliary triangle. Having drawn the circle, we proceed in the same way with villages 50 and 70; we get a second circle and the intersection of both circles gives the location of the school.

129

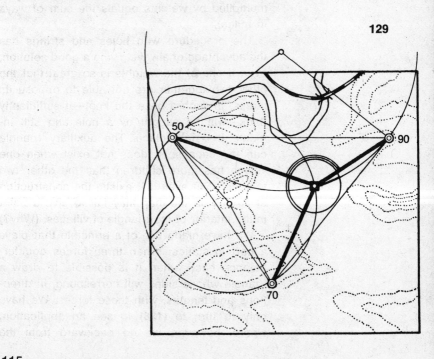

As to the first device of weights and holes, it results from the laws of statics that the equilibrium of the system of weights is possible only when their center of gravity is as low as possible. This center moves up or down when we change the length of a string by displacing the knot; its vertical displacement is proportional to the increase of the piece of string beneath the table multiplied by the weight it carries. Thus, the center of mass is as low as possible when the sum of the products of the pieces of strings above the table by the attached weights is as small as possible. But this happens exactly when the sum of the ways to school is smallest, because this sum equals the sum of the products of length of string and weight (we can assume one inch on the map for a mile in reality and one ounce for a child—then the sum of lengths of string multiplied by weights equals the sum of ways in miles).

The procedure with holes and strings has the advantage of always giving a good solution, even if one of the weights is so great that the other two together are not able to oppose its stress. In such a case the knot—if sufficiently thick—will be caught by a hole and still indicate the right place. The auxiliary triangle can fail because it does not exist when one village has more children than the other two together. But even if it exists, the construction of circles on the map may fail to give a point in the interior of the triangle of villages. (Why?)

We have made use of a principle that plays a part in statics: When three forces counterbalance each other, it is possible to draw a triangle whose sides will correspond, in directions and lengths, with those forces. We have only to turn to (128) to see an application, where, however, we go backward from the triangle to the forces. This remark leads to the so-called reciprocal figures of Cremona. If we have, for example (**130**), 10 rods bound together by pins at points *A, B, C, D, E, O*, we obtain 6 areas: 1, 2, 3, 4, 5, 6. Now let us draw the reciprocal figure (**131**) or the scheme of forces. The areas will now be indicated by letters, the vertices by numbers. In (**130**) the vertex *C* is common to areas 2, 3, and 6 and unites the rods *BC, OC, DC*; in (**131**) the area *C* has 2, 3, 6 as vertices and adjoins the areas *B, O, D*, the boundaries *BC, OC, DC* being parallel to the rods *BC, OC, DC* of (**130**). The whole scheme is constructed in like manner. Supposing that, at joint *C* of the rods, forces act in the direction of the arrows, their magnitudes being equal to the corresponding sides of the triangle *C* of the scheme, they will be found to counterbalance each other. The principle applies to other points of junction. For example, the forces at junction *D* are determined by the sides of the area *D*, but the arrow in rod *CD* now points toward *D*, because, by the principle of equality of action and reaction, the rod pushing *C* pushes *D* with the same force. Thus having drawn first the arrows in

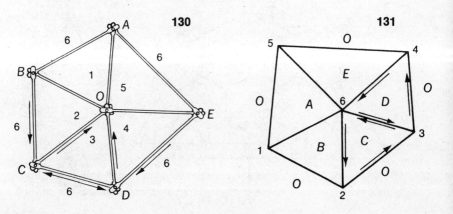

the area *C* of the scheme, we have to draw the arrow 6-3 in the area *D* contrary to arrow 3-6 in area *C*; as the arrows in every area have to form a circuit, we get all the arrows in *D*, then in *E*, and so on. Thus we can make out the whole scheme, provided we know the length of one side and the direction of the corresponding arrow. Hence it follows that, knowing one tension of the construction (**130**), we can find all the others. When this tension changes, it is only the size, not the shape of the scheme, that will change. Hence we see, for instance, that rod *OE* is always subjected to a force 26/15 times as great as that to which rod *BC* is subjected, and is pulled if *BC* is compressed. (Why?) When seeking the location for the school, we started with the scheme of forces and then found the shape of the system of linked rods in equilibrium (the strings were our rods).

Sketch (**132**) exhibits only a half of a bridge; we see the proper arch (upper belt), the beam

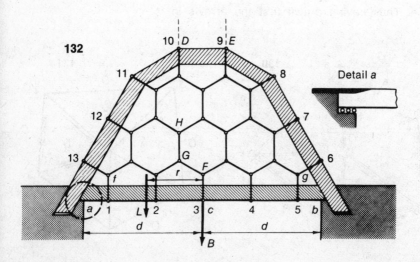

132

Detail *a*

(lower belt), and the hexagonal framework connecting these belts. The framework consists of 38 bars identical in all respects. They form a net of 16 meshes. Five of them are regular hexagons; border meshes are truncated hexagons, but the bars enclosing such meshes are no different from the others. The important feature is that the bars are connected by joints around which they are free to turn; this pivoting applies also to the 13 terminal joints; one can consider them as holes in the belt to make bars free to turn round the hole.

In spite of this individual freedom the framework of 38 bars behaves as rigid. To prove it let us remark that any deformation of a regular hexagon which keeps the lengths of bars diminishes its area: it follows that every deformation generates a pattern of a total area smaller than that defined by the sketch. Now, the total area enclosed by the arches cannot change. This contradiction shows the stability of the construction. This stability implies an equality of strains in all bars. This strain may change in time but it is the same in all bars. What happens if a heavy object of weight W appears at an arbitrary place of the lower beam a-b? The answer is simple: the strains in all bars increase by the same amount, which causes the strains to be equal still. For example, if we hang a weight W on rope CB, the strains increase in all bars by $W/5$.

The advantage of such a bridge is to have a framework of identical bars, the tensions in which are always mutually equal.

Analogous to the problem of the location of a school (**127**) is the question of the location of a telephone exchange, which has to be chosen in such a way as to use the least possible amount of cables for wiring.

Sometimes it is very difficult to find the

shortest path. Let a camp consist of several tents; the commander wants to choose a tent for himself in such a manner that, starting from it, he would be able to pass all the tents in as short a time as possible. If the number of tents is small we may solve this question by examining all possibilities, but if the number of tents is as high as 50, this method would require the work of many years. We invite the reader to help the professionals!

Let us pose an easier question: the tents are to be joined by paths, so that we can go from one tent to another; we have to make the total length of paths as short as possible, and, the paths are not allowed to cross each other except at the tents. In order to solve this we proceed as follows: We choose any tent, for instance *A*, and join it with the nearest one —on our sketch (**133**) it will be tent *B*—and we join tent *B* with *C* which lies nearest to *B*. From tent *C* we get no further, the nearest tent to *C* being again *B*. Thus we begin anew with tent *D*. The tent nearest to it is *E* and again our drawing stops. We choose again a new tent and proceed in this way until no tent is left. To get from tent *A* to tent *D* we must connect 'groups of tents' with each other. To connect group I with group II we draw the dotted path, it being the shortest distance between group I and II. The nearest group to II is III, and we join them also with a dotted line. Continuing, we get a system of connecting lines, similar to a railway network joining cities. This system of connecting lines we call a *dendrite*. The dendrite drawn here for towns (**134**) is only of limited interest: an ordinary map informs us already not only about the distances of the towns connected, but also about all distances between them—any drawing of lines is superfluous.

133

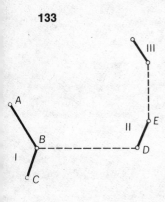

There is, however, valuable information to be derived from the town dendrite. For instance, if somebody would like to connect all principal towns with railways in the shortest possible way, avoiding crossing points outside the towns, the dendrite shown on sketch (**134**) will solve this problem.

Things are quite different with the objects to be treated now: they are not placed like towns on a plane, but in a space of many

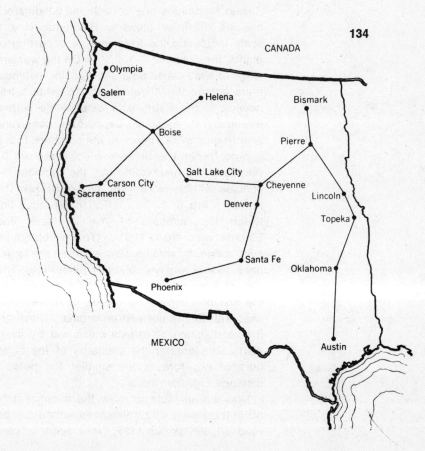

134

CANADA

Olympia

Salem

Helena

Bismark

Boise

Pierre

Salt Lake City

Carson City

Cheyenne

Sacramento

Lincoln

Denver

Topeka

Santa Fe

Oklahoma

Phoenix

MEXICO

Austin

dimensions (or characteristics). In producing a dendrite we proceed like a botanist who dries a flower expanded in space in a flat herbarium: he maintains only some of the most important distances between the particular parts of the flower—as does the dendrite.

We may speak of dendrites anywhere there are objects and distances—they need not necessarily be points on a plane. As an example let us choose 28 places in the forests of the Silesian Beskid Mountains and investigate the occurrence of certain species of moss, for instance, liverworts (Hepaticae). In the Beskid Mountains are to be found 31 different species of these mosses. Botanists have a scale indicating the frequency of occurring of plants, for example: 0, 1, 2, 3, 4. On the western slope of a hill called Smerekowiec, for instance, there occurs the *Alicularia scalaris* with a frequency 1, the *Cephalozia bicuspidata* with a frequency 2, and the *Cephalozia connivens* with frequency 0. Therefore the numbers 1, 2, 0 . . . correspond to Smerekowiec. There are 31 numbers, corresponding to the number of species of liverworts. On Wielki Stozek the numbers are 0, 1, 0 . . . The differences between the numbers of Wielki Stozek and Smerekowiec are 1, 1, 0 . . . This we obtain by subtracting the smaller numbers from the larger ones. In this way we obtain 31 differences. The sum of these differences may be considered as the distance separating Stozek from Smerekowiec. But this is not just an ordinary distance, it is a distance of forests measured by liverworts. The greater the similarity of the moss flora of two forests, the smaller the botanic distance between them.

Now we are able to draw the minimal dendrite. It consists of 27 distances, which can be read off our sketch (**135**). This dendrite cannot be drawn on an ordinary map, because the botanic distances have nothing in common with the ordinary distances of the places. You see small circles, representing the particular forests: black circles represent beech for-

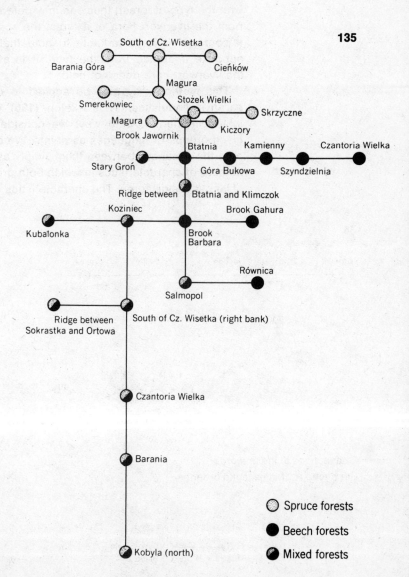

Spruce forests
Beech forests
Mixed forests

ests, stippled mean spruce forests, while half-blackened indicate mixed forests. Now it is interesting to see that differently shaded circles are not intermingled as a rule. This is a proof for the fact that the liverwort flora is linked with the type of forest; thus one may determine from the liverwort flora of a forest the species it contains. It is remarkable to note that the opposite inference from the type of forest to the liverwort flora does not hold.

This method may also be applied to comparative linguistics. Thus sketch (**136**) originates in the following way: we consider 11 given groups of languages as points. We compute the distances between them simply as the number of characteristics in which both groups of languages disagree. The characteristics used

136

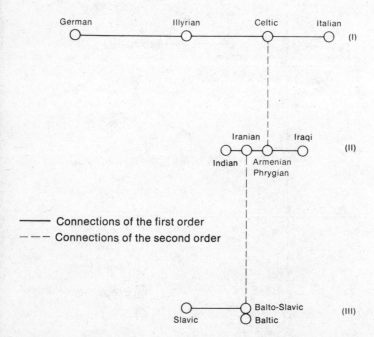

German   Illyrian   Celtic   Italian   (I)

Iranian   Iraqi   (II)

Indian   Armenian
Phrygian

——— Connections of the first order
— — — Connections of the second order

Slavic   Balto-Slavic   (III)
   Baltic

here were taken from a linguistic work. It can be easily seen how the dendrite divides the languages into the following four classes: (I) northwestern, (II) southern, (III) Oriental, and (IV) northeastern. This is a proof for the proximity of languages for nations dwelling near one another in the geographical sense. This method can also be used to classify human skulls (**137**), aircraft-motors, and many other objects.

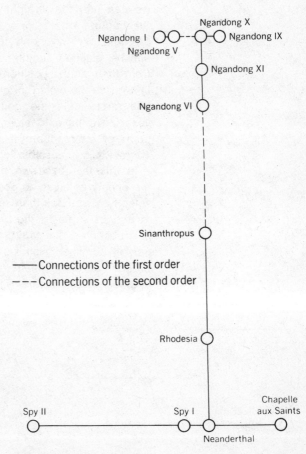

137

The problem of the shortest path arises when there is the question of pursuit. It is obvious that the best method of pursuit on an unlimited plane (ocean) is to take a course straight toward the object pursued. Nevertheless, the meaning of 'best method' is not immediately clear. If we know, for instance, that the vessel pursued does not know that it is the object of our pursuit, and that, consequently, it will keep its course whatever we do, we can do better than to steer right toward him. If we know the ratio $V:v$ of both velocities, we can find the straight course that assures the capture of our prey in the shortest time possible. We have only to find all points that can be reached simultaneously by both ships from their actual positions; they form a circle (**138**) (the so-called circle of Apollonius). If this circle cuts the course of the pursued vessel, we have to steer directly toward the point of intersection; if it does not cut the course, it is impossible to catch the fugitive.

In this last case we may try to approach the enemy as close as possible; supposing his velocity V greater than our v and his course at a right angle to the direction in which we first observed him (**139**), the simple construction of our sketch shows the best line of approach; at the moment of least distance the pursued ship appears right ahead. (Why?)

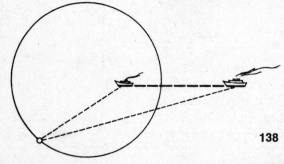

138

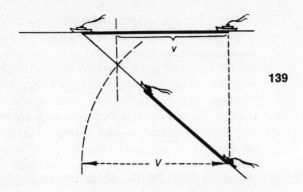

On the sketch this position corresponds to the black ship and the initial position to the white one. Should the sketch (**139**) be understood in the wrong way, attributing the speed *v* to the pursued vessel and *V* to the pursuing one (this mistake is compatible with the sketch), the drawing would still have a meaning. (Which?)

But it could happen that the captain of the other vessel takes notice of our design and changes his course; then the methods based on his ignorance lose their advantage. To define the 'best method' we must therefore reckon not with the best conditions but with the worst, as in chess and other games. Let us call the pursuer White, the pursued Black, the velocity of White *V*, the velocity of Black *v* and let *V* be greater than *v*. The efficiency of a method of pursuit can be measured by the time interval from the start to the capture; the shorter this interval, the better the method. On an infinite ocean, Black can keep to the simple 'rule of thumb': whatever method White chooses, to steer straight away from him. Then the relative speed of White, that is, the speed with which he approaches Black, will be $V - v$ or less, and the time necessary to capture will be $d/(V - v)$

or more, if d denotes the initial distance. Thus White cannot guarantee a shorter time than $d/(V - v)$, because Black, by using the rule of thumb, can enjoy his freedom at least during this time; he will remain free for a longer time if White does not always steer directly toward him. On the other side, White can guarantee to catch Black after the time $d/(V - v)$ at most; he has only to keep his prow always directed toward Black and to go full-speed ahead. He will make even better time if Black does not stick to his rule of thumb or if he reduces speed. Now we have the right to call the rule 'right ahead on Black' the best method for White and the rule 'right ahead from White' the best method for Black. When using his best method, White can guarantee the time $d/(V - v)$ but by no other method can he guarantee a better time. Black can, by using his best method, guarantee the time of freedom $d/(V - v)$, but by no other method can he guarantee a better, i.e. a longer, time. As the result $d/(V - v)$ is the same for both partners, the game of pursuit is a *closed* game. To realize how the pursuit can be considered as a *fair* game, we have only to stipulate that d, the distance, being measured in miles, V and v in knots, White has to pay to Black the amount $T - d/(V - v)$ dollars, T being the number of hours from start to capture; if the amount is negative, it is Black who pays. The game thus conceived is fair and—as we have already explained—closed.

The pursuit is more complicated if the encounter takes place close to shore (**140**). If the shore is approximately a straight line, however, we may proceed always by reading the old rule of 'right ahead' as the order to steer always toward the farthest point of the circle of Apollonius determined by the two ships. On the open sea this retains the old meaning, but

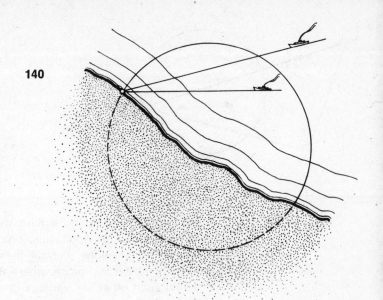

140

when the circle of Apollonius cuts the shore, the dry arc has to be erased and the farthest point on the circle refers to the wet points only. The circle moves with the ships but, so long as they adhere to the above rule, their course remains steady; it is directed toward the furthest point on the circle of Apollonius —in the new sense. It can happen that this point lies on the beach (**140**). In this case we may say that the ships are in the 'neighborhood' of the shore. This is advantageous for the pursuer—it reduces his guaranteed time to less than $d/(V - v)$ if he knows how to interpret the general rule. If he does not, and turns the prow directly toward his enemy who is clever enough to apply the improved rule, the point of Apollonius will wander along the beach delaying the capture. Nevertheless the pursuer is still guaranteed the time $d/(V - v)$. (Why?)

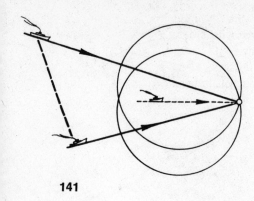

141

For two ships pursuing a third we have to trace two circles of Apollonius, one for each pursuer. The positions of both pursuers and the farther of the two points where the circles intersect each other are vertices of a triangle. If the escaping ship is in the interior (**141**) of the triangle, the best method for all three ships is to point toward the third vertex; if the fugitive is beyond (**142**) the triangle, the best method for the pursuers is the standard method of steering toward the prey; as to the fugitive, he has to compute the time of capture by the formula $d/(V-v)$ for both pursuers, to decide which danger is more imminent and to fly straight away from the more dangerous ship.

142

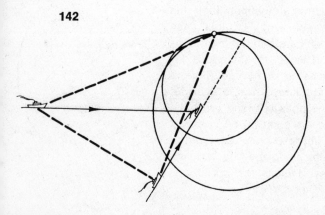

It is to be remembered that the triangle changes and the fugitive may cross its sides. This cannot happen if the fugitive has been initially in the interior and all three ships keep to the rules; in this case all ships will have a steady course. (Why?) The problem of two pursuers has not been solved by a complete mathematical reasoning; it is for the reader to prove or to disprove the results above; it is an interesting question, whether the definition of 'surrounding the enemy' given by situation (**141**) is correct.

Suppose one ship pursues another and keeps always a constant angle with the line connecting both ships, and suppose the fugitive does the same, steering at a certain constant angle from the connecting line. Then both will travel on curves winding themselves round a common (**143**) vertex. To find this vertex, which is obviously the point of capture, we trace the circle of Apollonius for the initial position of both ships, and another circle passing through these positions, and the point where their

143

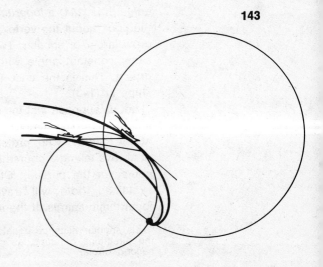

directions meet. The circles cut each other in two points; the farther one is the vertex sought for. The radii joining the vertex to the ships make angles with their directions, which are the same for both ships; this follows from the vertex lying on the second circle. The distances from ships to vertex have the ratio $V:v$ because the vertex lies on the circle of Apollonius. It follows therefrom that the triangle ship-vertex drawn for the initial position and the one drawn after a short time with the initial vertex are similar; the bases of the triangles are at both times the lines joining the ships. As the ships keep both their angles against this base, it is obvious that the relative situations of the ships and of their directions to the vertex are similar at both times; as V and v are constant, the new vertex will consequently cover the initial one. Viewed from this point, the angular distance of the ships will remain constant,* and the paths will cut the radii issuing from the vertex at a constant angle, the same for both. Now, we have a name for a curve cutting the radii at a constant angle: it is (**144**) a *logarithmic spiral*. If we turn the book about the vertex, the spiral seems to grow larger or smaller. Two spirals having the same constant angle with the radii are congruent. This is the case for the two paths of ships in (**143**).

Let us suppose that the captain of the pursuing ship is doing his best, i.e. pointing straight at the enemy, who prefers the pirate's trick of always taking a course at right angles to the course of the pursuer. Of course, as already explained, both will travel along congruent logarithmic spirals. If the initial distance was d

---

*This angular distance equals the angle formed by the directions of ships, as can be seen from the second circle.

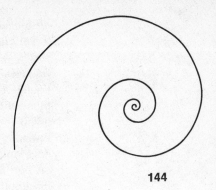

144

and the velocity of the pursuer *v*, the time
elapsing from the start to the moment of capture is *d/v*, whatever the velocity *V* of the
fugitive may be, because the fugitive's speed
does not contribute to the mutual distance.
The length of the spiral from its vertex to the
initial position of the pursuer is therefore *d*.
This being true at any moment, the length of
the pursuer's spiral from its actual position to
the vertex always equals the distance from ship
to ship. The ships always subtend a right angle
at the vertex (because the angular distance
equals the angle formed by the directions of
the ships, as can be seen from the second
circle). Is it possible (**145**) that both ships may
trace the same path? The answer depends only

145

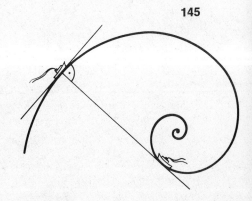

on the ratio V/v. If it is 3.644, both ships will travel on the same path and—what seems very strange—the fugitive, whose speed is greater, wanders on the far-water of the pursuer and finally collides with him. The logarithmic spiral thus obtained has the peculiar property of being its own evolute: it can be traced by a thread winding itself on the same spiral. We have only to consider the line joining the ships on our sketch as a thread of invariable length, the greater ship winding it round the spiral, as she travels along the next coil of the same spiral. The vertex is always 70° 40′ away from the prow.

A smuggler's ship perceives midway to the shore a boat patrolling the coast. The boat turns off its lights and the smuggler has to choose the nearest way to the point where his companions are waiting for the cargo. As he is three times as fast as the patrol boat he can do it without the risk of being surprised by his invisible opponent. The procedure is as follows (**146**). If C is the circle of Apollonius

146

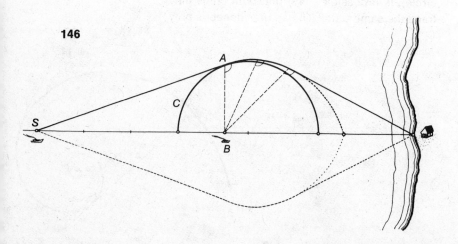

for *S* and *B*, the ship can surely take any steady course avoiding *C*. If, however he chooses the course along the tangent he reaches a point *A* on the circle; in this moment his course makes a certain angle with the line *BA*. He continues to sail under this angle against the fictitious fixed point *B* and he proceeds along the logarithmic spiral until he perceives right ahead the point he has to reach; then he goes astern. Thus his way is composed of two segments and a spiral arc. This way, however, is exactly on the rim of danger. To be always on the safe side, the smuggler has to draw his course exactly as told above but under the assumption of his own speed being a little less than it really is. Having drawn it, he sails along with his true speed—the pointed path is the safe one. (What happens if he assumes a speed 25 per cent beneath the true one?)

A simple device for drawing logarithmic spirals consists of a ruler sliding along a nail; a sharp lamina compels the pencil to move, always making the same angle with the ruler **(147)**.

147

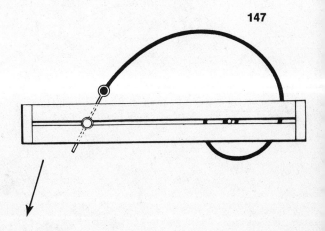

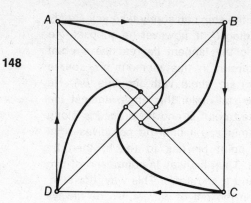

148

Four dogs *A, B, C, D*, forming initially a square *ABCD*, start to run all at once with the same speed: *A* toward *B, B* toward *C, C* toward *D, D* toward *A*. Eventually, they meet all in the center of the square. The path of each (**148**) is a spiral of the same kind as in (**144**), (**145**). The length of each path is equal to *AB* as already shown. The spirals cut the diagonals of the square at an angle of 45°. (Why?) What if there were only three dogs forming an equilateral triangle?

149

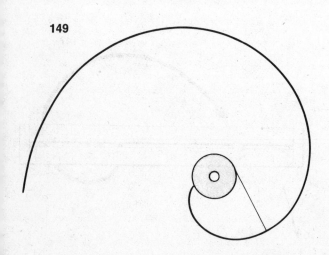

In unwinding thread from a round bobbin there arises another kind of spiral (**149**): the evolute of the circle. If we can imagine an object suddenly freeing itself from the laws of gravitation (and resistance of the air), we should see it flying away from us and describing exactly the same spiral. (Why?) Supposing a fly crawls along the radius of a uniformly revolving gramophone record with a uniform velocity, it will be describing another kind of spiral, the so-called spiral of Archimedes (**150**). Here the length of the radius-vector is proportional to the angle of that radius with a fixed direction. A heart composed of two arcs of such a spiral (**151**) and fixed upon the face of

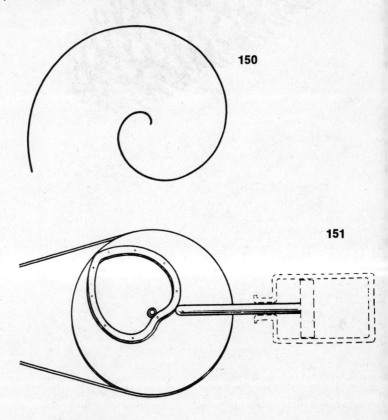

150

151

a disc will change the uniform, rotating motion of the disc into the uniform, to-and-fro motion of a piston. (Why?)

When looking at pine cones one easily perceives the arrangement of their scales: it is a spiral too (**152**).

152

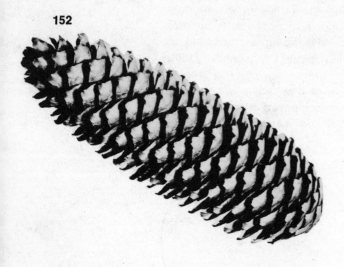

6

Straight Lines, Circles, Symmetry, and Optical Illusions

A polygon made of rods may assist us in drawing a straight line without the help of a ruler. The *inversor* (**153**) consists of six rods, of which the four shorter ones are equal and form a movable rhombus, while the two long ones —also equal—connect two vertices of the rhombus with the fixed point F_1. When the other fixed point F_2 is joined to the third vertex of the rhombus by the seventh rod—equal to F_1F_2 in length—and all junctions are movable, the free vertex, when we deform the rhombus, traces a straight segment.

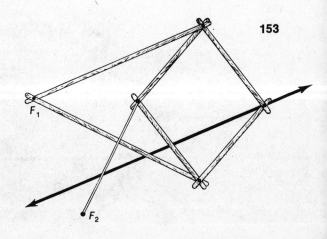

153

F_1

F_2

To determine the centroid of a stick, we place it horizontally (**154**) on the edges of our palms and then we bring our hands closer together; finally (**155**) they meet in the center of gravity. The stick never loses its equilibrium because when the centroid, which is initially between the palms, approaches one of them, the pressure on the nearer palm becomes many times greater than the pressure on the other palm; its product by the coefficient of

friction must finally surpass the analogous product for the other palm; when this happens, the relative movement of the first palm ceases and the relative movement of the other one starts. This play continues alternately until both palms meet; the centroid is always between them and it is there at the final stage. The trick is done automatically without any conscious effort.

Any construction for the tracing of which the compass and ruler are used may be drawn without the help of the ruler. If, for instance, we wish to find the center of a segment 1–2 (**156**), only the ends of which are given, we draw circles with a radius 1–2 from point 1 and from point 2, and find their intersection 3. Then with the same radius we trace a circle from that point, which gives the point 4. Still with the same radius, we draw another circle

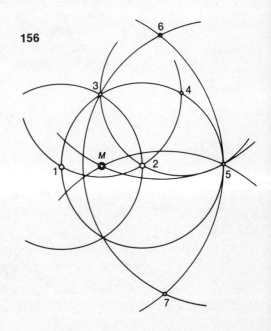

156

(through 3 and 2), which intersects the second circle at 5; from 5 with radius 5–3 and from 1 with radius 1–5, two further circles are drawn which intersect each other at 6 and 7; from these points through 5 we draw two circles whose intersection M is the desired center. The figure has 8 circles. (Can there be fewer?)

Given two intersecting circles, we can find (**157**) their centers by means of the ruler alone. We choose point a on one of the circles; through an intersection of the circles and point a we trace a straight line and find point b. Then we return from b through the other intersection to c. Starting from A instead of a, we find in the same manner B and C. We now join a to c and A to C, also A to a and C to c, using dashed lines, and thus obtain the points S and T. The line ST (dotted and dashed) passes through the center of the circle $AaCc$; repeating the construction with another point, we obtain a second diameter and the center. (How many lines are necessary?)

If we use only a compass and a ruler, it is impossible to get a construction that will give the circumference of a circle, if the radius

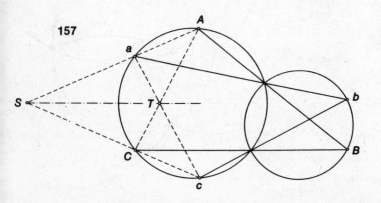

157

is already given. The ratio of the circumference of a circle to its diameter is 3.141592653. . . . Father Kochański, a Polish Jesuit, gave the following approximate construction (**158**): From point *A* on the circle we draw another circle with the same radius and obtain 1; from 1 we trace a circle with still the same radius to obtain 2; the line joining 2 to the center *O* intersects the tangent drawn at *A* in point 3. By measuring off a triple radius upon *A* from point 3, we get 6, and the segment *B*-6 is approximately equal to one half of the circumference. (With what approximation?)

If we draw all possible circles through two points (**159**), there exists a second series of circles meeting them at right angles. This second series consists of Apollonius' circles (cf. (**138**)).

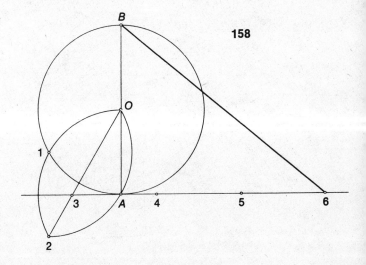

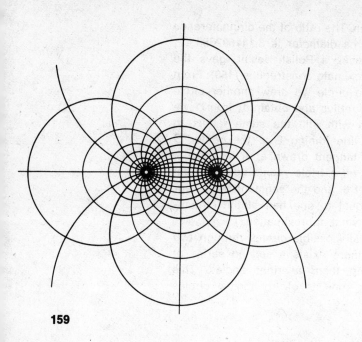

159

160

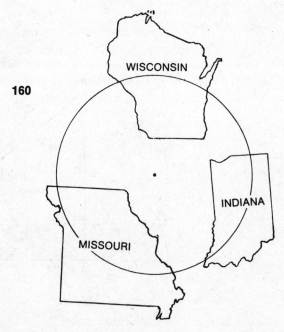

144

Three domains of arbitrary shape and situation being given (**160**), it is always possible to halve them all by a circle. To halve two domains a straight line is sufficient. The corresponding property in space is the 'sandwich theorem': it is always possible to cut a sandwich with a plane stroke so as to halve the bread, the butter, and the ham.

If we roll one coin along another of the same size (**161**), the point of contact will run along the circumferences of both the moving and the fixed coin. The circumferences are obviously equal; hence if the point passes along half of the circumference of the fixed coin, it will pass half the circumference of the moving coin. But on testing this system, we find that the moving coin again lies heads up. (Why?)

Copernicus states that if a circle rolls along the internal circumference of another circle whose diameter is twice as long, each point on the circumference of the smaller circle describes a straight line (**162**). Let us consider

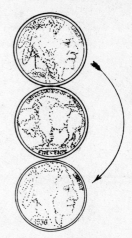

161

162

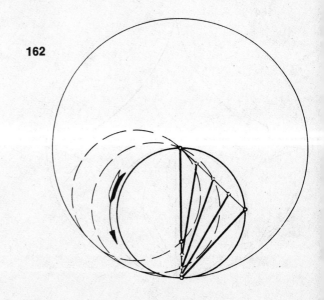

a match fixed as a chord to the small circle and watch its movement from the moment when the head of the match touches the large circle till the moment when the other end reaches the center of the large circle. The match has swept the area of a right triangle, and every point of this area has been touched only once by the match. Therefore every triangle can be swept with a corresponding movement of a match (**163**).

163

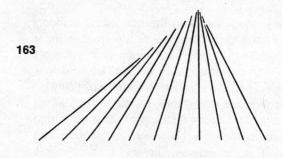

164

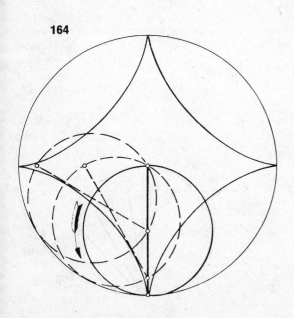

Conversely, if we move a match so that both ends of it travel on intersecting straight lines, the movement can be obtained by the Copernican system of rolling a circle in another twice as great. The center of the large circle lies at the point of intersection of the given straight lines, and the small circle is given by the ends of the match and the center of the large circle. It passes through these three points (and keeps passing through them during the whole movement) (**164**). This experiment fails when the match equals the diameter of the small circle; it then sweeps out the interior of an astroid.

When a wheel rolls along a straight line (**165**), a point marked on its circumference (nail *P*) describes a *cycloid*. At every moment, each point of the circumference moves toward the highest point or away from it, the speed being proportional to the distance of the moving point from the lowest point. (What is the velocity of the lowest point?)

165

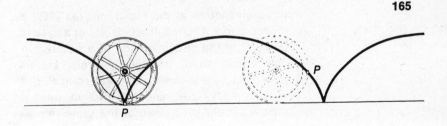

Let us suppose another circle, twice as great, rolling with the same speed as the given circle, and let us mark its diameter, which was vertical at the start: it always touches the cycloid beneath, gliding on it (**166**). By fixing the point nearer the center, we obtain (**167**) a curve without cusps, and when we fix it upon

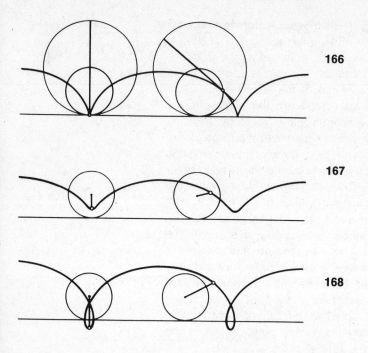

166

167

168

the prolongation of the radius, we get (**168**) a looped curve. The length of the arc of a cycloid is equal to the circumference of a square circumscribed about the rolling circle. Let us turn (**165**) upside down; then the point *P*, if it were a heavy ball and the cycloid were a groove, would slide down at the same rate as if an invisible generating circle traveled with a uniform, rolling motion along the horizontal road above, with the ball attached to its circumference. A ball falling along a cycloidal groove (**169**) precedes one falling along the inclined plane, even when it must return upwards. Our sketch shows an inclined plane (dashed line); and shows also the position of the ball on the plane at the moment when the ball moving along the cycloid crosses the

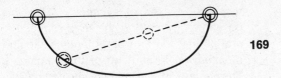

plane. Such calculations are greatly facilitated by the fact, remarked by Kant, that points falling along inclined planes and starting from the same spot (**170**) simultaneously form a circular arrangement at any time. The ball falling along the cycloidal groove reaches its goal faster than along any other curved groove.

A circle has the largest area of all closed curves of the same circumference. Hence the area of a field, enclosed by a curved line of the length L, is never greater than $L^2/4\pi$. (Why?) The area enclosed by curves different from a circle can always be augmented without changing their length; if a curve has two

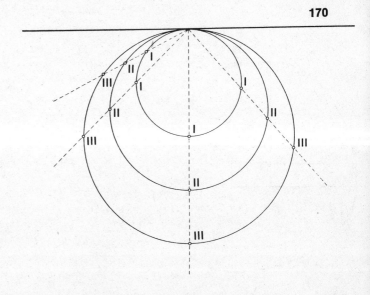

rectangular axes of symmetry (**171**) this can be shown by cutting the area along the axes and putting the four parts together again (**172**), after having turned two of them upside down. The square in the middle shows the increase of the area; the circumference is obviously the same as before.

A circle has constant breadth: we can roll a round disc upon the table without the hand rising or falling. But there are other figures

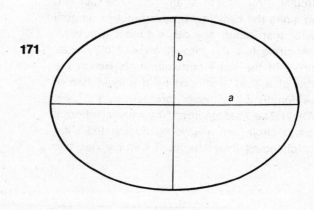

171

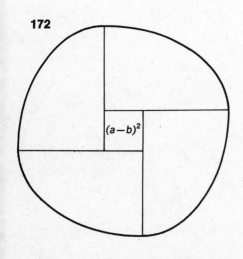

172

$(a-b)^2$

of constant breadth. If we draw circles around the vertices of an equilateral triangle as centers with radii equal to its sides, we get also (**173**) a closed curve of constant breadth; if we wish to have it smooth, we have only to prolong the sides of the triangle equally (**174**) and draw six arcs of circles, using again the vertices as centers, but describing the arcs alternately with a radius equal to the prolonged side and a radius equal to the prolongation. A curved line so constructed keeps, when rolling, its highest point on the same level. A line of constant breadth has the same length as any other line of the same constant breadth; the longimeter obviously gives the same measure in both cases—which can be considered as a proof. The length is equal to breadth times 3.14159.... (Why?) A closed curve can rotate in the interior of a triangle, touching always all sides. In the case of an equilateral triangle the smallest area having this property is a lens-shaped figure (**175**) enclosed by two congruent arcs of a circle whose radius is the height of the triangle.

173

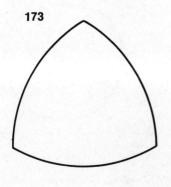

174

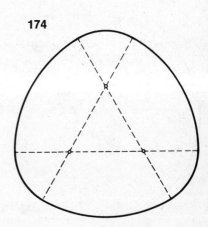

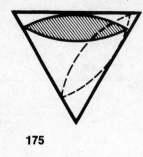

175

Figure (**175**) suggests the problem of whether a convex curve that is not a circle can roll inside a square. This problem finds an immediate answer, given by (**174**).

Related to the same topic is the possibility of a noncircular convex curve such that a fixed equilateral triangle can be inscribed in it and moved so that the corners of the invariable triangle describe the curve simultaneously. Such curve is to be seen in (**176**). It can be considered as the section of a cylinder and the triangle as that of a rotating piston. When compared with ordinary pistons moving back and forth along the axis of a cylinder in gasoline motors, the rotating piston is considered to be a great improvement. The fact that curve (**176**) is not a circle makes such technical application possible. Why?

If all chords of a curve passing through a given point are equal, the curve need not be a circle, as can be seen by sketch (**177**). However, if there is no longer chord in the curve it is necessarily circular.

176

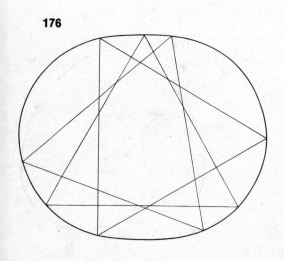

177

An arbitrary convex curve being drawn, there is always a star of six rays enclosing angles of 60° and such that the opposite rays are equal. We believe the theorem to be true for any closed curve: we have tried it here on Lake Superior (**178**).

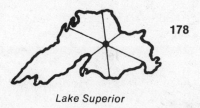

178

Lake Superior

A circle has the property that a rod of a homogeneous material lighter than water, of circular section, may float motionless on water, no matter how we turn it round the axis. The contours given here (**179**), (**180**), have the same property, if we assume the density of the material of the rod to be 1/2 the density of water;

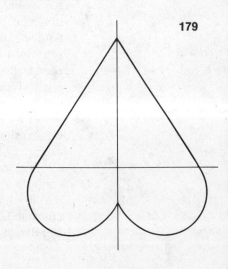

179

they are so calculated that every chord halving the circumference also halves the area. This property is not peculiar to curves with a center like (**180**). This second solution of the floating problem is seen to have three axes of symmetry and three straight segments as parts of its contour.

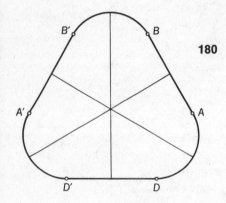

180

Some soldiers have been ordered to start from point *P* (**181**) and halt 30 paces behind the trench. Each of them chose a different direction, and, upon halting, they formed a bent line, the so-called *conchoid of Nicomedes*. Afterward they were commanded to return 60 paces, then 30 paces more, then 30 paces again. Thus a second line was formed (the full line on the sketch), a third with a cusp, and a fourth with a loop; the lines with dots indicate where the soldiers found themselves after executing the first and last maneuvers.

A similar experiment with a circular trench leads to *Pascal's limaçon*. (**182**) In this case the lines arising after the first and second command (30 paces beyond the trench and 60 back) make a single smooth curve, crossing itself.

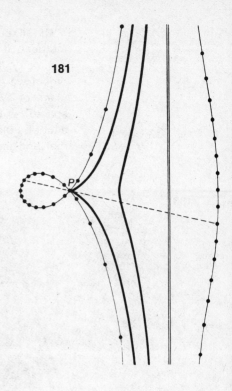

181

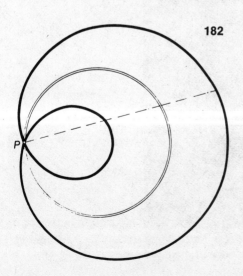

182

Of all curves the circle is the most symmetrical: it has an infinite number of axes of symmetry. To get a symmetrical replica of any object we can use a mirror. The mirror is the plane of symmetry. Placing a circular disc in space, let us consider its image in a mirror and let a plane pass through the centers of the real and imaginary discs so as to cut out of

183

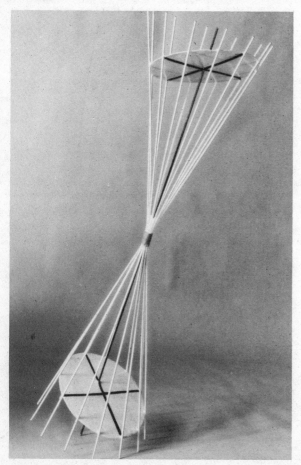

them the diameters maximally inclined toward the mirror. By joining (**183**) the endpoints of these diameters crosswise, we find a point on the mirror. If we make this point a vertex of a cone having the real circle as its base, we shall see another cone in the mirror. Both cones can be considered as one, because the generating lines of the real cone give, when prolonged, the generating lines of the imaginary one. Thus we get the construction of our photograph; the mirror has been removed. The straight line, however, which joins the center of one disc to the vertex of the cone, does not pass through the center of the second disc, as the black wire of our model clearly indicates. (It is easy to verify this statement by cutting the model by the auxiliary plane mentioned above and by reducing it to an obvious fact of plane geometry; the figure obtained consists of three wires and two diameters and is visible on our photograph.) (**183**) This fact proves the impossibility of constructing the center of a circle by using only a ruler. For if such construction were possible, we could, by drawing it on the plane of one circle and projecting it through the vertex of the cone on the plane of the other circle, obtain a second construction, executed strictly according to the same rules, because the intersections of straight lines pass into intersections. This is true also of the intersections of the straight lines with the circle. Hence the center of the first circle, being one of these intersections, should pass into the center of the second circle, but that is not the case. This proof of impossibility is highly characteristic of mathematics.

To make a plane picture of a three-dimensional object, we appeal to *geometrical perspective*. A camera furnishes it automatically but the ancient masters employed the same means to obtain the impression of perspective depth. **(184)** Horizontal parallels always meet on the 'horizon-line' of the picture; if they are perpendicular to the background, their apex is the 'principal point' (marked here by a small circle). Only by placing the eye on the perpendicular to the picture issuing from the principal point does one get, without deformation, the visual impression corresponding to the three-dimensional reality.

The optical illusion of a portrait following with its eyes a spectator walking along is easy

184

to explain. In the case of a living immobile model (**185**) the view changes as we walk along: first one ear disappears behind the head, then one eye begins to hide behind the nose, and so on. Only if the model turns its head to watch us frontally, do we continue to see both ears, both eyes, and so on. Now, with a picture we always see both eyes and both ears, whatever our point of view; thus the portrait makes the impression of a person's turning his head to look at us.

 **185**

On a summer afternoon the author saw a swarm of little flies dancing, as mosquitoes do, in one place and then flashing quickly to another place some yards away to dance there in pairs and to return after a minute or so to the old place and to repeat the same play again and again. This game lasted long enough to allow him to determine roughly the velocity of the jump; it was about 40 miles per hour. When looking attentively, he could see on the track of the jump (**186**) sparkles of light; they

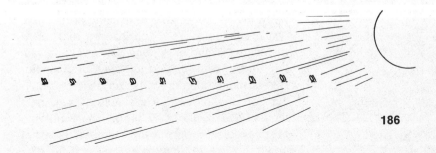 **186**

formed dotted lines and were approximately half an inch apart. It was obviously the effect of the sun shining sidewise on the insects; they became visible only when their wings were lifted and illuminated by the sun. Every rosary of sparkles belonged to one single fly and their plurality was only an illusion resulting from the permanence of the images on the retina. Forty miles per hour is about 700 inches, which equals 1400 half-inches, per second: it follows that the frequency of beats of flies' wings was 1400 per second; allowing 40 per cent for error of estimation, we can summarize the observation as giving a thousand or more beats per second. It is curious that such a computation can be made without instruments.

For a fly, one beat of its wings is the same as one step for a man. A man makes two steps —a fly beats its wings 1600 times per second, i.e. its life flows 800 times faster; a single minute for the fly means the same as 12 hours for man. Thus we may compare the above cycle with a dance in the morning and in the evening.

The notion of symmetry leads to the following toy. On a horizontal table we place a vertical frame carrying a transparent sheet of glass (**187**); it divides the table into left and right parts. We turn a small screw into the right part of the table. When doing it we see somebody turning a screw into the left part: obviously, the glass acts as a mirror. We now put a mark on the table at exactly the position of the fictitious screw, and insert a real screw there also. This being done we cover the real left screw with a clod of clay of diameter several times the screw; for an observer looking from the left side of the table there is only the surface of the clay to be seen, but the observer placed on the right side will see not only the clay but also the screw, as if the clay

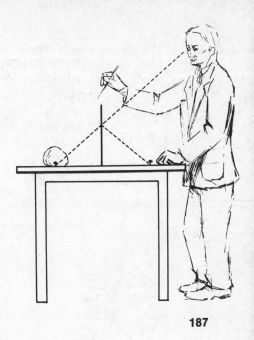

were transparent. Reaching beyond the vertical frame with his lancet, he can easily touch the head of the screw immediately, through the clay. He sees the screw without seeing it!

The idea described above can be used to locate foreign bodies (e.g. fragments left in the human body by shrapnel); for such purposes X rays have been applied with success since Roentgen discovered them in 1895. In 1938 a method was published which combines the X rays with the advantages of the toy above. To avoid misunderstanding let us mention that between 1895 and 1938 at least 200 methods were proposed; many efficient ones among them had the drawback of holding patient and surgeon under X rays during the operation, in spite of the danger implied by such permanent exposure.

The sketch (**188**) shows the vertical cross section of an operating table with patient fastened to it; the screen above and the X-ray lamp beneath are rigidly connected by a rod parallel to the line defined by the lamp's focus and the midpoint of the sensitized screen *S*, marked by a crossing of fine lines ruled on the plate, which we shall call 'the cross.' Suppose a grain of shot (*P*) to be the objective of the operation; it is always possible to shift the table with the patient so as to put the grain on the line defined above: we will recognize it by seeing the shadow of the grain on the cross.

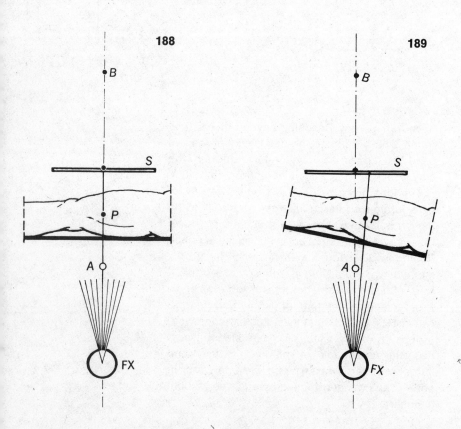

188

189

The next step is to turn the rod around the horizontal axis A by an angle of 15° or so. If this displaces the grain from the cross we have to restore the grain-cross effect by shifting the axis A with the whole system up or down; if turning the rod does not destroy the alignment, no moving of A is necessary. A look at both sketches (**189**), (**190**) may convince the reader that the brilliant point B (e.g. small electric bulb) is now located symmetrically to the grain P, the screen being the plane of symmetry. The last step is to replace the screen by a sheet of glass G. This being done

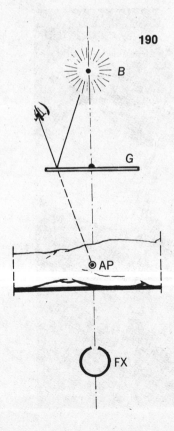

190

we can apply the idea of our toy. We cut off the X rays and switch on light in the room: the surgeon can boast that he could touch the grain with his lancet if it were necessary. An important advantage of this method is the absence of X rays during the operation: neither the surgeon nor the patient is exposed to them (**191**).

Recently an important improvement has been put forward for consideration. Instead of the electric bulb B, three thin sticks S_a, S_b, S_c converge to B at 60° angles. The sticks are

191

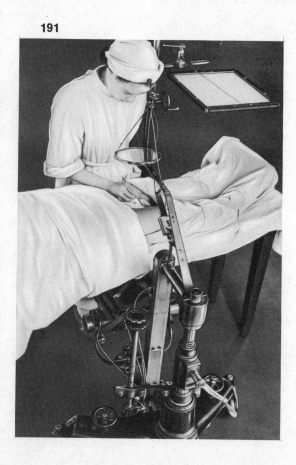

different colors, and each of them carries a tiny ring. The surgeon looking through the glass (**191**) 'sees' not only their apex at *P* under the skin of the patient, but also three sticks piercing the patient's skin; the surgeon can shift the rings so as to 'see' them on the skin, and he marks these points *a, b, c* on the skin with their respective colors. This being done he is free from all X-ray apparatus. Let us suppose that the surgeon is compelled to adjourn the operation to another day and to an operating room having no X-ray equipment. He can do it easily: the patient being immobilized on the table, the surgeon sets up the glass and installs the tripod so as to bring the rings *a, b, c* into juxtaposition with their respective colors on the patient's skin when he looks through the glass. The surgeon will then "see" the apex at *P*. The mathematical background of this proposal is obvious.

Some optical fallacies are of a very startling character. When viewing a fence of wire of the kind in (**15**), page 10, it happens occasionally that we are deceived as to the distance of the fence and we fail to grasp it, reaching too short. To evoke this phenomenon we first look at a point in front of the fence and then suddenly draw our attention to the fence, without changing the direction of our eyes. The explanation is that, because all squares of the fence are alike, we have no guide to tell us which of the left-eye images corresponds to a right-eye image. If we identify two images of two different squares crosswise and attribute them to a real square, we locate this square on the crossing of the lines of vision—which brings the fence closer to us than it really is. It is also possible to push the fence back, but this is more difficult. (Why?) The difference between images of the same object seen with the left and with the right eye is the chief factor for stereoscopic vision. To get pictures that convey the stereoscopic impression, the method of anaglyphs draws suitable sketches in perspective. Anaglyphs are two projections of the real object, one from the center of the left, another from the center of the right pupil. The first is red, the other green-blue; looking at them with two-colored spectacles (red glass for the right eye and green-blue for the left), we shall see a three-dimensional picture. (Why?)

A very simple optical fallacy hinders our estimating the distance of a horizontal wire without visible poles sustaining it. The reason is the homogeneity of the wire. If there were a red spot on it, we should direct both axes of vision on the spot and immediately get the perception of distance; if there is no such mark, it is sufficient to incline the head on one shoulder. (Why?)

7

Cubes, Spiders, Honeycombs, and Bricks

Nature realizes cubes in the shape of salt crystals (NaCl) (**192**); we can fill the whole of space with them. A cube may be painted in 30 different ways, with 6 colors, a different one for each face. If we have 30 such models and take any one of them, we can find 8 other cubes and build of the latter a larger cube in such a way that the colors of the adjoining faces will be the same and that the arrangement of colors on the large cube will be exactly the same as that on the small one.

192

Of the six pieces in (**193**) we can form a cube (**194**), a process that is by no means an easy task. There are two solutions. If the cube's edge is 3 inches, there are among those pieces three composed each of 5 little cubes with one-inch edges, and three composed each of 4 such little cubes. Two pieces are congruent by symmetry. (Was it possible to avoid it?) By putting the pieces together in the way indicated here (**195**), we get a beautiful architectural design (**196**). The number of different designs which can be assembled is so large as to occupy the entire life of one person.

193

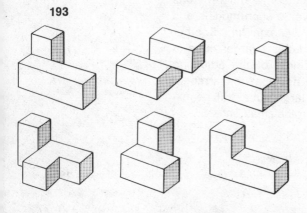

194

195

196

A cube intersected by a plane halving the long diagonal and perpendicular to it gives for section (197) a regular hexagon. We also get a regular hexagon when we view from above a cube whose long diagonal is perpendicular to the (198) horizontal plane of projection.

197

198

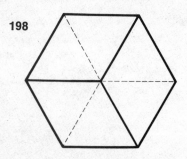

According to Pohlke, one can draw any three segments from one point, complete the figure with (dashed) parallel segments, and (199, 200) consider it as a (generally oblique) projection of a cube.

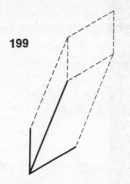

199

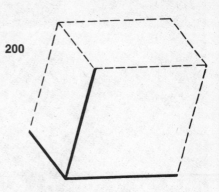

200

Twelve rhombi of the same shape and size can be placed together so as to form two hexahedra of different shape and size; their surfaces, however, have equal areas (**201**).

201

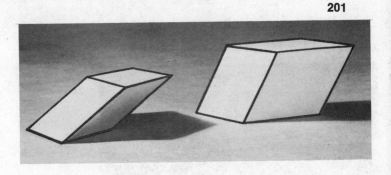

If we make a model cube of white wire (**202**) and then take several photographs of it on the same plate, turning it before taking each view, round the long diagonal by the same angle, we shall obtain a picture (**203**) composed of two cones and a hyperboloid of revolution. (The photograph shows clearly the hyperbola that is the meridian of that hyperboloid.) The hyperboloid is a surface composed of two families of straight lines.

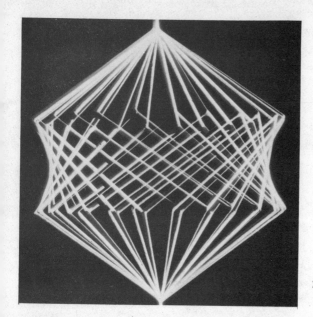

202

203

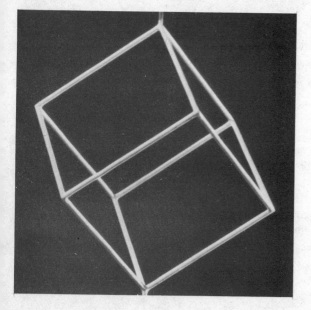

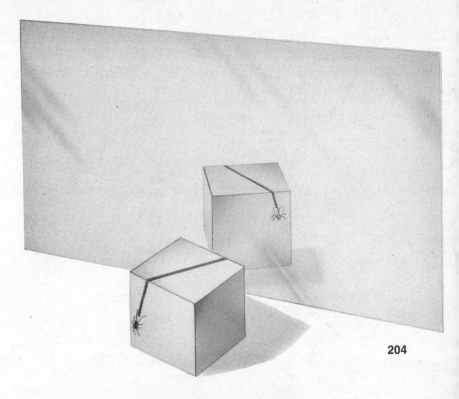

The straight line is the shortest path. We can make use of this rule to determine the shortest route on a cube. When a spider sitting on the cube (**204**) wants to catch a fly sitting on another face, it will find the shortest way in the shape of a straight line upon the diagram (**205**) of the cube. If the fly wishes to make sure that there is no spider on the cube and, leaving its position, wants to crawl over all the faces of the cube and return as quickly as possible, its route on the diagram (**206**) will also be a straight line. It is likewise apparent from the diagram that the point of departure does not affect the length of the circuit (**207**). The fly has, however, the choice of two different ways. The shortest circuits cover the

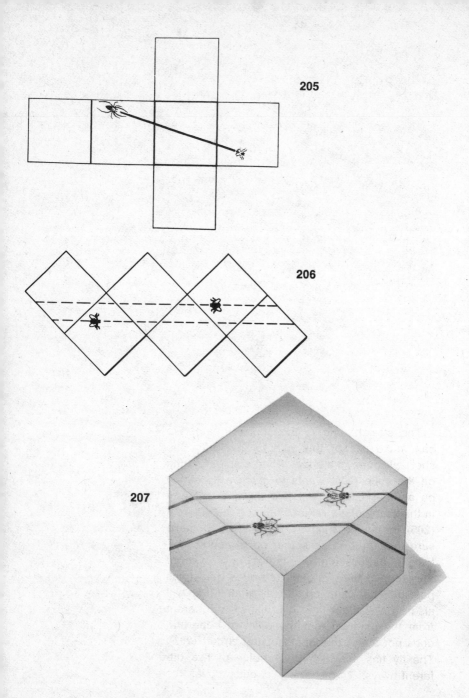

205

206

207

whole cube with lines (hexagons) of constant length, two such lines passing through every point. Would it be possible to make one family of these lines of white thread and another of red thread, so as to get on each face of the cube a two-colored fabric, the threads of the same color being parallel? No, 4 colors are necessary. (Why?)

If we weave every family with threads of different colors we will get as many hues as there were pairs of colors, i.e. 6 (through each point pass 2 threads). On each face there will be 4 hues; each hue occupies a triangular-shaped quarter of the face. (Is each face differently colored?)

The diagram (205) can be applied to another question. Let us consider A, B, C, D as the corners of the bottom of a cubical stone, and the square without letters on the corners as the upper face of this cube. A fly sitting on the midpoint P of an upper edge asks the reader: 'I would like to go as far as possible on the stone; what is the farthest point, and the shortest possible path to it?' $APDEFA$ (208) is a closed tour. The distance CD is 1/6, assuming edge = 1. $APD = \sqrt{4 + 1/36} = 2.0067$. By suitably 'unfolding' the square and laying the faces flat in such a way that $DEFA$ forms a single straight line, it is easy to calculate that $DEFA$ = 2.0067 also. Does the point D answer the question that the fly asked the reader?

Every point on the cubical stone has a point farthest from it, but not every farthest point is symmetrically opposite: the midpoints of opposite edges are not farthest from each other. Let us call such points transitive points. The sphere has no transitive points. Are there other convex surfaces without transitive points?

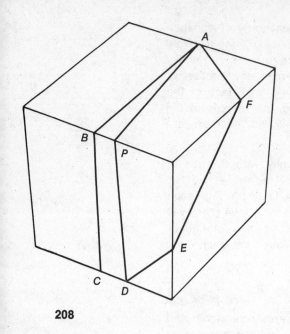

208

Some chocolate shops present their wares in boxes bound by an oblique ribbon forming an octagon (**209**). This octagon can be shifted without altering its length—which shows that there is a whole family of parallel geodesics on such a box. This gives a solution for a fly going round the box, other than those pictured on (**207**).

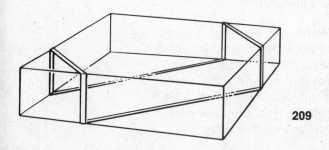

209

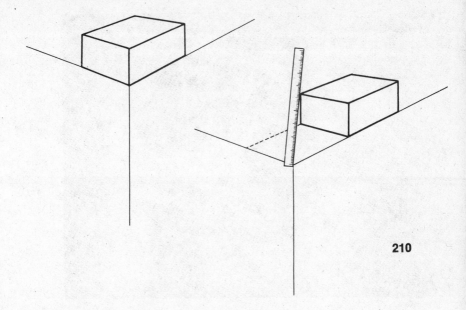

How can we measure the great diagonal of a box with a ruler? (**210**) gives the answer to this.

The photograph (**211**) shows a cube of pasteboard; it is deprived of base and cover and its interior surface is black. Each of the four remaining faces consists of 4 triangles; thus we have 16 equal triangles. The strips connecting them flexibly are easily visible. Proceeding with the cube (**211**), we manage to turn its inside out as shown by the series of photographs (**212-217**), reaching eventually the situation (**218**), which gives a black exterior to the same model.

Taking a rectangle of paper of a length four times its breadth, one can glue together the short edges, getting thus an open cylinder. The question how to turn it inside out without tearing the paper has already been answered (**211-218**). How to achieve the same if the circumference is only thrice the height of the cylinder is a more intricate problem.

211

212

213

214

215

216

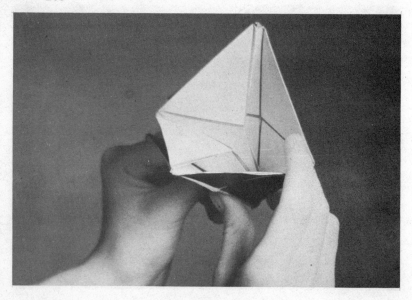

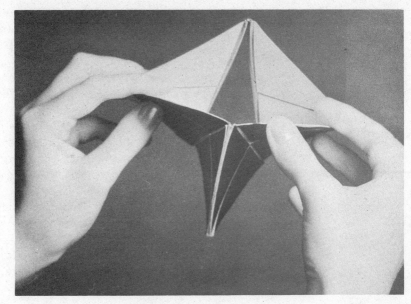

To find shortest paths we can sometimes proceed as with the cube: spread the surface, on which the path is to be traced, on a plane, draw a straight line, and bend the model back to its previous shape. For instance, a cone is a surface made up of a group of straight lines. A fly, wishing to take a turn round the cone and get back to where it was as soon as possible, would follow the loop (**219**) that returns to the starting point at an angle. The cone, cut along one of the straight lines (**220**) and laid open, would present a sector, and the fly's route would consist of two lines perpendicular to the sides of the sector. If the cone is equilateral or even more blunted, the solution is a different one: the fly walks straight to the top, takes a look round, and comes back the same way.

219

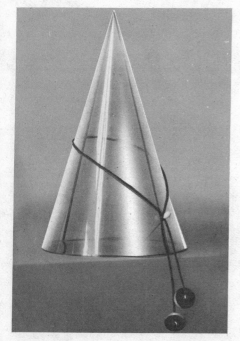

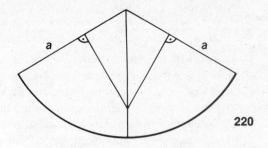

220

There are surfaces that cannot be spread out as can the cone; the sphere is such a surface. The shortest lines on the sphere are the great circles, the so-called *orthodromes*; every meridian is such an orthodrome. Let us suppose we could spread out, without stretching, the sphere's surface on a plane. All the orthodromes would conserve their lengths and become shortest ways on the plane, and thus they would become straight lines. On the other hand they are closed, while straight lines are not. This fact shows the impossibility of spreading the whole sphere on the plane. But even when we try to spread a part of the sphere, the part of the earth's surface that lies north of the polar circle, for instance, we encounter an absurdity: the meridians converging in the North Pole (**221**, **222**) become, when spread

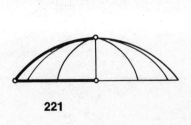

221

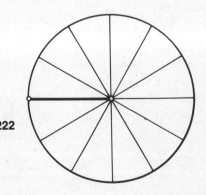

222

out, straight segments of equal length and the whole cap becomes a disc whose boundary is a circle. This circle is the polar circle, which conserves its length too; the radius of this circle is equal to the radius of the polar circle —which is to be seen on the plane cutting the sphere in the polar circle, whereas the distance from the North Pole measured along the meridian (drawn as a heavy bent line on the sketch) is obviously greater. The radius of the cap when spread out must therefore be equal to two different segments at the same time— which is absurd.

Some cartographers propose to project the surface of our globe on the icosahedron whose twenty triangles are tangent to our sphere. The center of the sphere would be the center of projection. Discarding the 4 triangles nearest to the South Pole and cutting the polyhedron along three edges (**223**) we can put 16 triangles on a horizontal plane; the central point is the North Pole. The advantages of this procedure are that the distortion of a triangular map of a size of 1/20 of the globe is the same for all triangles, and that the 4 missing triangles in our map refer to the almost uninhabited part of the earth.

223

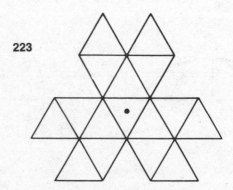

We have already mentioned filling the whole of space with cubes. We can get another filling of this sort by the following procedure: we make the cubes alternately black and white to get a kind of chessboard and then we remove the black ones. We decompose each void space into 6 pyramids on square bases with a common vertex in the center of the void space. If we consider a single white cube (**224**) with 6 pyramids based on it, we see a rhombic dodecahedron with a cube inscribed in it; it is obvious that by our procedure we have filled the whole of space (**225**) with congruent rhombic dodecahedra. It is very easy to find the volume of such a dodecahedron: we have used 2 cubes to build up one dodecahedron, and it has therefore twice the volume of the cube, $2a^3$, if a is the edge of the cube. The shorter diagonal of the rhombic faces is a, the longer one $a\sqrt{2}$, thus the sides of the

224

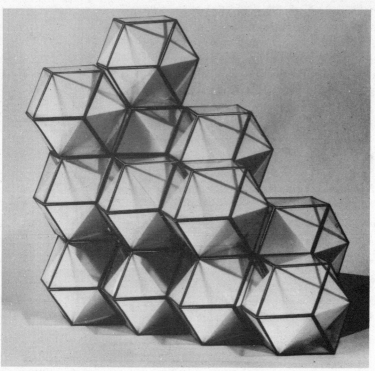

225

rhombi are $b = a\sqrt{3}/2$, and the volume $2a^3$ of the solid equals $16b^3/3\sqrt{3}$. The vertices are of two kinds: (1) where 4 solids meet; (2) where 6 solids meet.

The cells in a honeycomb can be obtained from two layers of dodecahedra by replacing the free faces (3 in every dodecahedron) by a hexagonal aperture (**226**); thus, there are in every honeycomb points where 4 cells meet and points where 6 cells meet.

There is an interesting question involved in filling the space with congruent polyhedra so as to have only 4 meeting in every vertex (it is impossible to have only 3). To find such

226

polyhedra, let us consider the bricks in a wall extending indefinitely in all directions. When laying the first layer, we shall stick to the mason's rule of thumb to block interstices by adjoining bricks (**227**). We notice that the first layer (full lines on the sketch) is not an es-

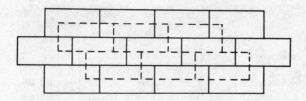

227

sentially new tessellation of the plane; if we consider every point where three bricks meet as a vertex, we see that every region is a hexagon, and the whole only a distortion of the honeycomb pattern of (**71**), page 75. Laying a similar layer on the first (dashed lines), we want to cover every vertex by a brick. Thus we get four bricks meeting at every vertex. Laying a third layer on the second, we place it exactly over the first and repeat the procedure indefinitely. Let us count how many neighbors each brick (**228**) has. There are 6 in the same layer, 4 above, and 4 beneath it, a total of 14. Let us imagine the neighbors' edges painted black and gradually decompose our masonry (**229**), (**230**) to see on the white brick the black traces left by the edges of adjoining bricks. We see 14 domains, left by 14 neighbors. Thus the brick is a 14-hedron, squeezed to the shape of an ordinary brick. To find the undistorted shape, let us remark that we find on the brick 6 'squares' and 8 'hexagons.' This observation leads to the truncated octahedron (**231**). It is our distorted brick and fills the whole space (**232**) in such a way that only 4 solids meet in each vertex; it is semiregular—which means that its faces are regular polygons. There is no other solid having these properties and thus it gives the simplest decomposition of space in congruent parts.

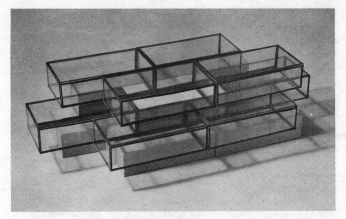

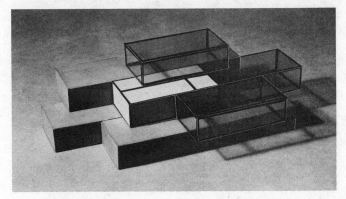

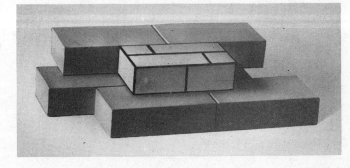

231

232

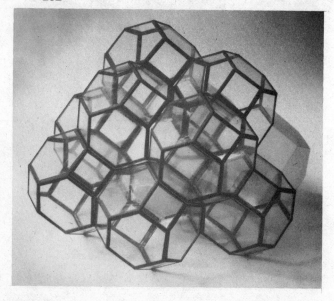

8

Platonic Solids, Crystals, Bees' Heads, and Soap

Plato knew that there were only five regular polyhedra. How can four triangles be made from six matches? To do it, it is necessary to make a basic triangle with three of the matches, and with the remainder form the three edges of a pyramid. Thus arises (233) a regular tetrahedron, the first of the Platonic polyhedra. It looks like (234) when projected vertically on its base, and another projection can give a square with diagonals (235). The model can be obtained from a flat diagram (236). After painting the four faces of a tetrahedron with different colors and rolling the wet

233

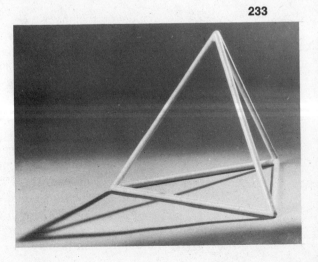

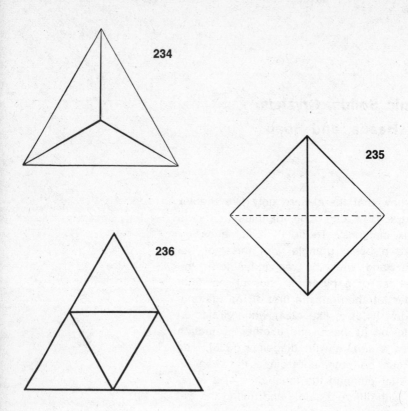

234

235

236

model on a plane, we get the tessellation (**237**). It is a remarkable fact that by rolling the tetrahedron to and fro in whatever direction one likes, the colors will never intermingle. (Could you do the same with an octahedron painted in eight colors?)

The second Platonic body, the cube, has already been shown. It is possible to build a larger cube from 27 equal cubes. Blackening the faces of this cube and cutting it up again into smaller ones, there is a certain number of cubes with three blackened faces, others with two, still others with only one, and again others not blackened at all. How many are there in each group?

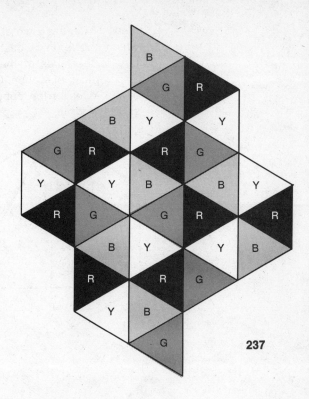

237

From eight equilateral triangles (**238**) it is possible to compose the third Platonic body, the regular octahedron. By placing it on one of the triangular faces and projecting it on the

238
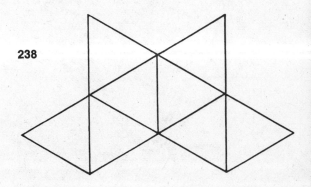

plane of the base, we obtain the drawing (**239**), which shows (thick dashed lines) that the centers of the faces of the octahedron (**240**) are also vertices of a cube. Conversely, the centers of the faces of the cube (**241**) are vertices of an octahedron.

239

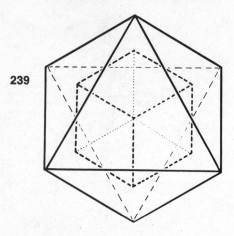

240

The next Platonic solid, a regular dodecahedron (**242**), has pentagonal faces. From the diagram (**243**) we can easily obtain a model. We have to pass the point of a knife along the edges (on the side of the cardboard that has to become the exterior of the model); then we place one star crosswise on another (**245**) and bind them by passing an elastic thread alternately above and beneath the corners of the

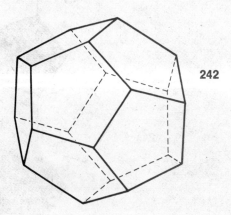

242

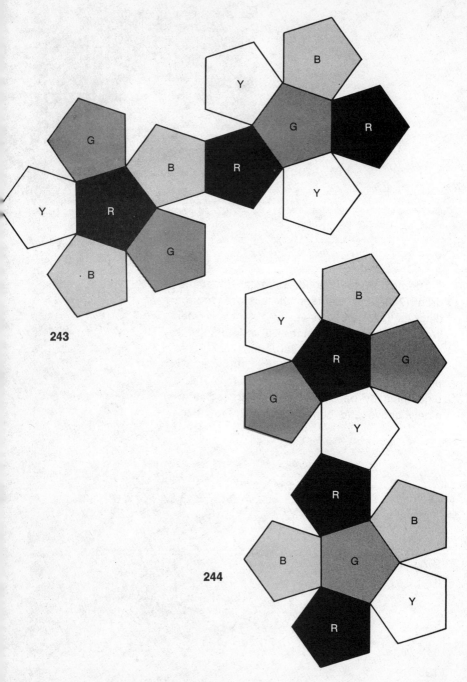

243

244

245

double star, holding the model flat with the other hand. Removing the hand (**246**), we see the dodecahedron rising (**247**) as a perfect model. To paint its faces so that adjoining faces have different colors, no less than four colors are sufficient. Choosing four colors, e.g. red, green, blue, and yellow, we may distribute

246

247

them on a dodecahedron either as illustrated by the sketch (**243**) or in an essentially different way (**244**). (By rotation and reflection can we transform one of these models into the other?)

We can inscribe a cube into a regular dodecahedron in such a manner that every edge of the cube becomes a diagonal of a face of the

248

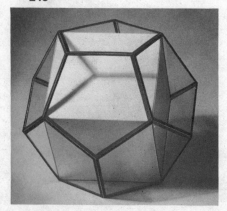

dodecahedron (**248**). This we can do in five different ways—the five cubes constitute a new stellar polyhedron. The space, however, common to the five cubes is a 30-hedron (**266**).

The last of the regular solids is an icosahedron. Its diagram (**249**) is composed of twenty equilateral triangles. Its horizontal projection (**250**) can be combined with that of the dodecahedron (**251**); in fact the centers of the faces (**252**) of the dodecahedron form the vertices

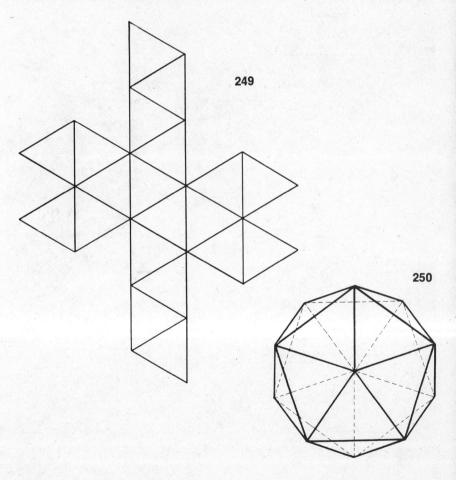

249

250

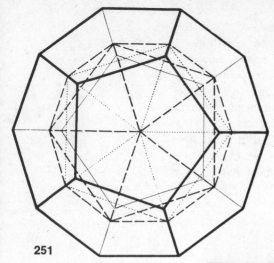

251

252

253

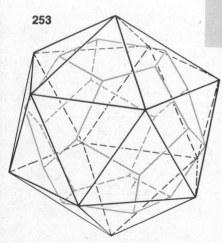

of the icosahedron, as our model proves. Conversely, the centers of the faces of the icosahedron form the vertices of the dodecahedron (**253**), (**254**). Only the tetrahedron corresponds to itself, as the centers of its faces (**255**) are the vertices of another tetrahedron.

255

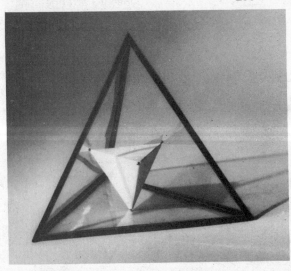

Balls of equal size do not fill a space. The same principle applies to circles in the plane (**256**): their densest possible distribution reminds us of the honeycomb and we can well imagine how the circles when squeezed would become •hexagons. The densest arrangement of spheres can be obtained by dividing the whole of space in cubic cells (without walls but with edges of wire) by calling them alternately black and white and placing in every white cell a sphere as large as possible. Thus only half of the cells will carry spheres and it will be easy to compute the ratio of the part of space occupied by spheres to the whole space. There is one sphere for each pair of cubes; the cube's edge being a, the radius of a sphere is half the diagonal of the square a^2, that is to say $a\sqrt{2}/2$. The volume of the sphere will be therefore

$$4/3 \cdot \pi \cdot (a\sqrt{2}/2)^3$$

and the volume of the pair of cubes being $2a^3$, the ratio is $\pi\sqrt{2}/6 = 0.7403$. Thus the densest arrangement of spheres occupies

256

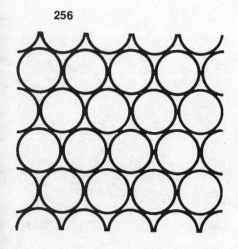

about 74 per cent of the whole space. Thus, if we have a soap mixed with gasoline, the soap's proportion being more than 75 per cent, we are sure that the gasoline cannot form a medium in which the soap is suspended in little spheres; we know that it is the gasoline that is suspended in the soap. Thus the emulsion will not be inflammable and its domestic use involves no danger. An emulsion containing more than 75 per cent gasoline certainly is inflammable—what can be said about an emulsion, with 50 per cent gasoline?

There is another way leading to the densest arrangement of spheres. We place first a layer of balls on the plane in such a manner that viewed from above, they look as shown in (256). Now we place a similar layer on the first, putting each ball of the upper layer into a hollow formed by three balls beneath it. Notice that balls cannot be placed in two adjoining hollows. Therefore if we place now a third layer upon the second, we may do so in such a way that its balls come to lie over the hollows of the first layer left free by the second layer (257). We may also dispose them otherwise (258), viz. so that its balls lie over the balls of the first layer. In both cases each ball of the middle layer is in contact with 12 neighbors. In the first method these points of contact are vertices of a cuboctahedron, the crystal of argentite (Ag_2S) (259), which arises by cutting off the vertices of a regular octahedron by a cube whose faces halve the octahedron's edges. In the second method they give the vertices of another 14-hedron (260) composed, like the first, of 6 squares and 8 equilateral triangles. If we halve it by passing a plane through the edges forming a hexagon, turn one half against the other 60°, and join the halves again, we obtain the cuboctahedron.

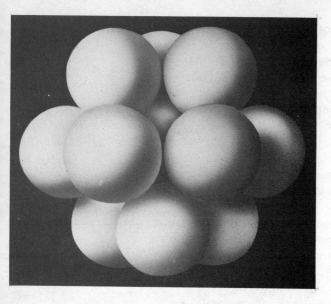

257

258

259

260

Now let us suppose that the balls are of yeast and that they rise equally. The gaps between them will fill up, and each ball will be transformed into a polyhedron whose faces will be found to be the common tangent planes of the balls. In the first case we shall get the rhombic dodecahedra of (**224**), (**225**), pp. 185-6, and in the second, solids (**261**) limited by 6 rhombi and 6 trapezoids. We can obtain the first solid from the second by cutting it along the equator and by turning the upper half 60° round a vertical axis. In this way we find both solids having the same volume, the same surface, and vertices of the same kind, while their faces have the same circumferences, the same areas, and the same angles. The first method of placing spheres shows also that the cuboctahedron can be inscribed into the rhombic dodecahedron; the second method gives an analogous result. (Which?) We have already seen how space can be filled with rhombic dodecahedra; it can be filled with the other

261

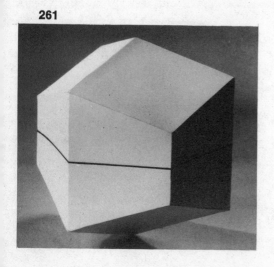

dodecahedra, as the experiment with yeast explains. Is this distribution of spheres identical with distribution (257) or with distribution (258)?

The cells of a honeycomb can be obtained by squeezing two layers of balls placed upon each other in the densest way. We thus obtain two layers of hexagonal, angular columns ending with trirhombic roofs; the roofs of one layer will be also those of the second. We might account for the origin of honeycombs by the action of elastic balls (in this case the bees' heads packed as densely as possible upon both sides of a thin wax slab).

One may ask, which filling of the space is the better one: that by dodecahedra (242, 247) or that by semiregular 14-hedra (259, 260)? The point in question is which is the more economic way, i.e. which requires less material for faces? The second way of filling the space (we have called it the simplest) is approximately about .6 per cent cheaper. In other words: if those bodies have the same volume, then the surface area of the 14-hedron is about 6 per cent less than the surface of the dodecahedron. It is remarkable that this extremely small difference may be perceived by inspection; one can see that the 14-hedron approaches closer the sphere, which—as we shall see later—is economically the best one.

The fluorite crystal (CaF_2) (262) resembles the truncated octahedron, our distorted brick of (231), page 190. The crystal of pyrite (FeS_2) resembles a regular dodecahedron (263). Other minerals crystallize in very interesting irregular forms: sphalerite (ZnS) crystals are dodecahedra limited by congruent deltoids (264); cuprite (Cu_2O) takes the shape of trisoctahedra (24-hedra) bounded by congruent irregular (265) pentagons. If we place a plane along each

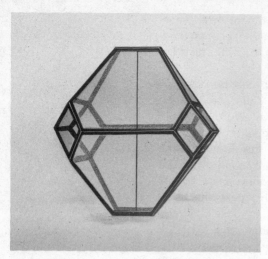

262

263

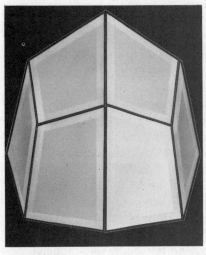

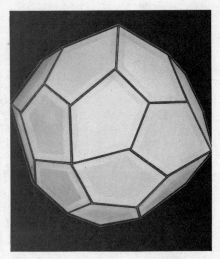

264

265

edge of a regular dodecahedron, perpendicular to the plane of symmetry in which this edge lies, we shall obtain (**266**) a rhombic triaconta-hedron (30-hedron). The diagonals of the rhom-

266

bic faces are the edges of regular polyhedra: the shorter ones give a dodecahedron, the longer edges an icosahedron. Proceeding with the triacontahedron as before with the dodecahedron, we get a 60-hedron. (What faces will it have?)

The problem of proportional polling solved in the plane for three political parties (**69**), page 72, leads, in the case of four parties, to a division of a regular tetrahedron by means of planes parallel to its faces and equally distant from each other (**267**). Employing an infinite number of planes in each of the four families of equidistant parallel planes, we get a filling of the whole space. It is a filling composed of regular tetrahedra and regular octahedra.

267

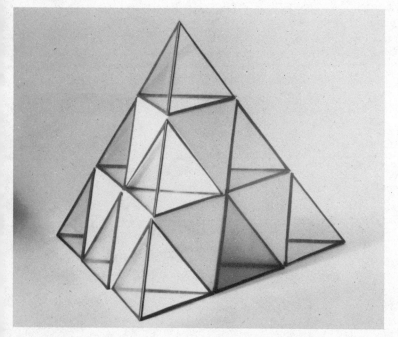

In addition to ordinary polygons we find the so-called 'stellated' forms. The stellated pentagon, (**268**) the 'pentagramma mysticum,' is the favorite figure of magicians and astrologers. There are three heptagons, (**269, 270, 271**) one convex and two stellated. This photograph (**272**) gives an idea of a polyhedron bounded by 12 stellated pentagons.

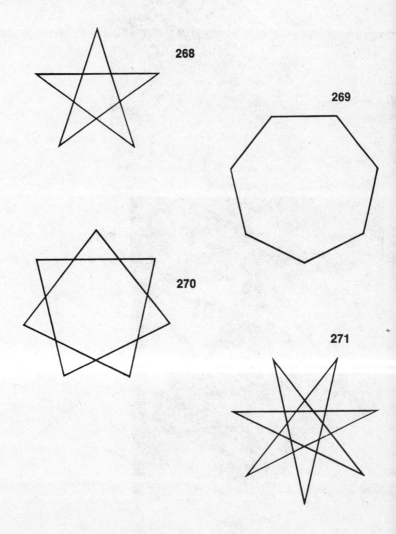

268

269

270

271

272

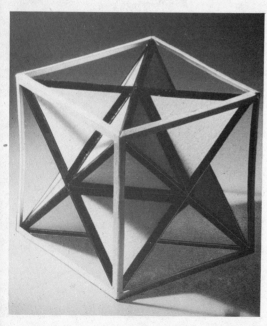

273

We can choose four vertices of a cube to be vertices of a regular tetrahedron. This can be done in two ways (**273**) and the two tetrahedra together give a 'stellated octahedron.'

The reader may explain the sketch (**274**), showing two cubes. How many faces has the polyhedron made of parts common to both of them?

274

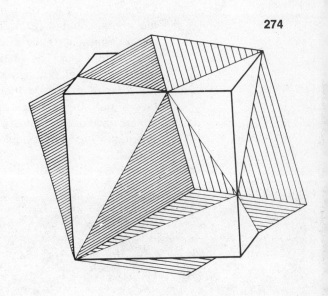

9

Soap-Bubbles, Earth and Moon, Maps, and Dates

The easiest way to obtain a sphere is by blowing a soap bubble (**275**). The surface tension of the liquid film tends to diminish the surface area of that film. The bubble encloses a certain quantity of air, hence the film assumes the form of a surface that, the volume being given, has the smallest possible area; the sphere is the only surface with this property. The moon was once a liquid ball; as every drop

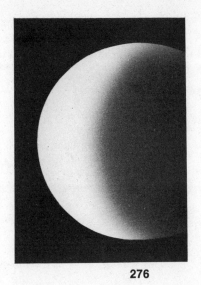

276   277

of the fluid attracted every other drop of the fluid mass, the drops arranged themselves in such a way that every change in the shape would require work. It can be proved that only the spherical shape has this property. The photographs (276, 277) show a balloon and the moon, both illuminated simultaneously by the sun.

If we take a pipe with two circular openings (278) and dip them in soap suds, we see, when we blow air in the pipe, two caps of film growing equally until they reach the shape of hemispheres. Then a strange thing occurs: one of them continues growing while the other one diminishes. The reason is the property of the sphere being the least area enclosing a given volume. After a certain amount of air has been blown into the pipe, the problem to be solved by nature is to enclose the surplus of air that exceeds the volume of the pipe's tube in as

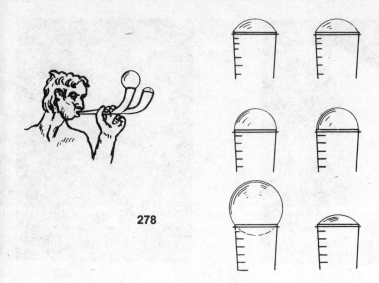

278

small an area as possible, with the condition that both bubbles are attached to the circular edges. The problem is the same as to enclose a given volume in a surface that has a part above the circular opening and another beneath it, because we can always put the two bubbles together without altering the volume and the area. As long as the amount of air is too small to fill a sphere with the pipe's mouth as equator, the solution is a symmetrical lens. This lens grows to a sphere, and from that moment there exists always a sphere, reposing on the pipe mouth, large enough for any given amount of air. Such a sphere is visible on our sketch with its lower part marked by a dashed arc; when we bring this part back to the other opening, we see why the second bubble decreases. (How?)

The earth has the shape of a sphere **(279)**. One of the black lines joining Lisbon to Cape

279

Farewell (the higher, i.e. the more northerly one) represents the shortest route between the two places. It is a great circle on the sphere, a so-called orthodrome (the meridians are also orthodromes; of the parallels of latitude only the Equator is an orthodrome). The second line is a loxodrome, i.e. a line representing a fixed course; it intersects all the meridians at the same angle. A sailor who has chosen a direction on the compass and keeps it steadily is following a loxodrome. The navigation becomes thereby much easier, but the voyage is longer.

We see that the loxodrome, when prolonged, coils around the Pole spirally and would be impracticable for an explorer of far northern waters. Mercator's projection (**280**) is a map that renders angles accurately; the meridians and the parallels of latitude form a rectangular lattice on the map, and the loxodrome is a straight line. It cuts all meridians on the earth at the same angle and must therefore do the same on the map. The meridians being parallel

280

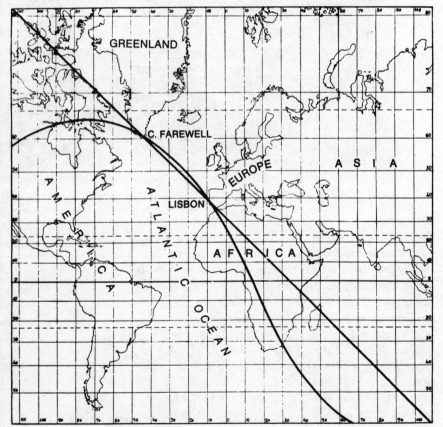

on the map, the loxodrome cuts parallel lines on the map at a constant angle; it must consequently be a straight line. The orthodrome on the contrary, shows here an inflection like a sinusoid (cf. (**304**), page 234). If we project the surface of the sphere from the South Pole upon a plane tangent at the North Pole (stereographic projection), we obtain a map that represents circles on the globe as circles and preserves angles (**281**). Thus on this map the

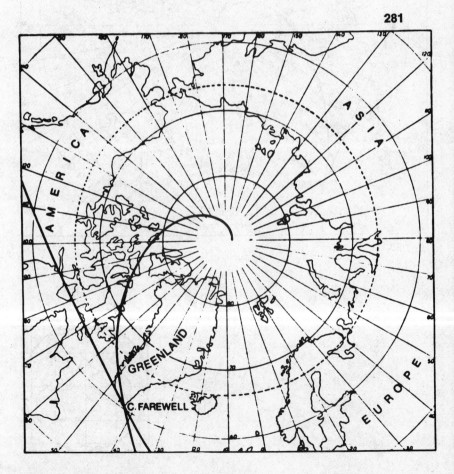

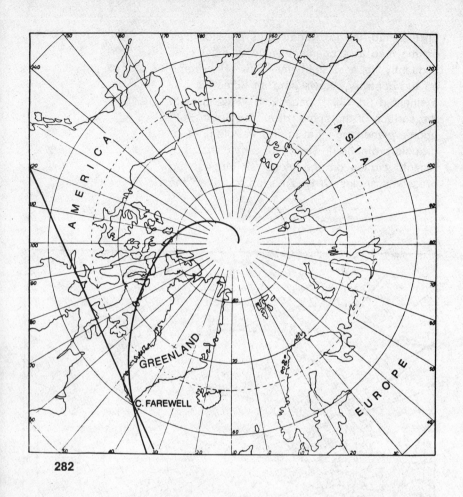

282

283

orthodrome appears as a circle (with a large radius) and the loxodrome as a logarithmic spiral. The last proposition results from the fact that on the map the meridians are evidently straight lines meeting at the Pole, and that the loxodrome is a line that cuts all of them at the same angle. If we projected the globe upon a plane tangent at New York from the antipodes of New York, the meridians and parallels of latitude would give (159), page 144.

If we project a sphere upon a plane tangent at the North Pole from the center of the sphere (gnomonic projection), the orthodrome (282) will appear as a straight line. Hence it is the most suitable map for flying in polar regions.

If we place a sphere in a cylinder touching it along the Equator (283), and if we project the sphere on the cylindrical surface by prolonging the planes of every parallel to cut the cylinder and do the same with all the meridian planes, we get on the cylinder a map of the sphere (284). By cutting the cylinder open and laying it flat, we get a map of the sphere with a rectangular and straight net of meridians and parallels. This map has the peculiarity (known to Archimedes) of conserving areas. If we then imagine the sphere covered with a thin uniform

284

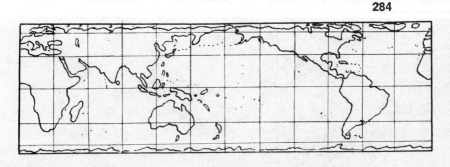

layer of paint or clay and bring every particle of it to its proper place on the cylinder, we shall get a uniform covering of the cylinder with matter; if we transfer it horizontally back to the common axis of the cylinder and the sphere, we shall cover the axis uniformly with matter. We could have covered it immediately, without the mediation of the cylinder. We can, however, do the same thing differently in two steps: first we project the matter vertically by a parallel projection, all particles falling freely down or going up on the Equatorial plane (**285A**), and we get a circular distribution (**285B**), then we project it again on a diameter of the Equator, getting of course a uniform distribution (**285C**). Thus we have found a distribution of matter on a disc that gives a

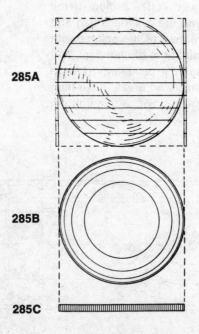

285A

285B

285C

uniform distribution when projected on any diameter of the disc. There is only one solution to this problem.

It was already known by Archimedes that the volume of the sphere is twice the volume between sphere and cylinder.

To explain the paradox of date on our globe, we can imagine the map (**284**) to be drawn on a transparent sheet and brought back to cylindric shape by being glued to a drum. One of the meridians separating Asia from America and passing through the Pacific may be used as the dateline (**286**). The time is shown in the form of a ribbon of paper drawn by a hidden cylinder of wood rotating inside the immobile

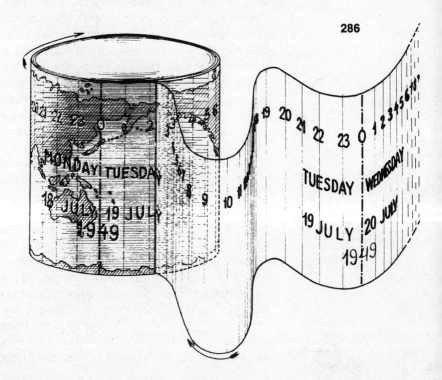

286

Earth; the ribbon crosses the transparent surface of the model through a fissure cut along the date line. The exterior part of the ribbon is the future, the coils already hidden are the past, and the part visible through the transparent map is the 'today.' Thus the ribbon is a sort of calendar carrying days, months, and years; they are separated by transversal lines and divided into hours. The midnights are transversal lines on the ribbon separating the days; as the date changes at midnight we always see on the Earth two lines of date: the fixed one and the midnight line. Thus we see here Tuesday extending from the fixed line to the mobile one that is west of the fixed line; beyond it, it is still Monday, extending westward from the mobile line back to the fixed line. As the mobile line wanders to the west, Tuesday increases in area and Monday decreases; finally there is a moment when Tuesday reigns the world over. But it lasts only a moment, because Wednesday comes and the midnight line leaves the fixed line of date, moving to the west and creating between itself and the line of date a narrow strip for the new day; Tuesday's decline begins and the game goes on and on.

If the earth were cylindrically shaped it would be possible to draw parallel circles and perpendicular to them meridian straight lines. Let us suppose that these lines were visible on land and sea. Then navigation would be greatly facilitated because on a cylinder the shortest lines (which are helices) cut the parallels and meridians at a fixed angle. On a spherically shaped planet it is impossible to draw such a network, cutting every great circle at constant angles. Besides the cylinder there are other bodies for which such perfected nets are possible. As we know, it is possible to cut a cone and develop it on a plane; on this the shortest lines become straight ones. Now on a plane an ordinary square net, as that of (**15**), has the following property: every straight line cuts the meridians and parallels at a constant angle. By applying this net together with the plane onto a cone, the problem would be solved. But there is still one difficulty to be overcome, viz.: in order to connect the lines smoothly along the seam we must choose the cuts properly before we start closing up the cone. We can choose (**287**) for the vertex angle A, 90°, 180°, or 270°. Thus three dif-

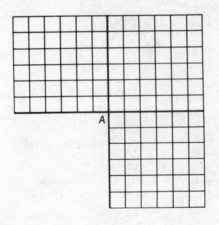

287

ferent cones arise. The first (**288**) has a net consisting of only one family of lines. Every line intersects any other and also itself once and only once. The second cone (**289**) has a net consisting of meridians and parallels, each parallel intersecting each meridian once and only once. The net of the third cone (**290**) consists of three families: we may call them parallels, meridians, and *paradians*. Each family

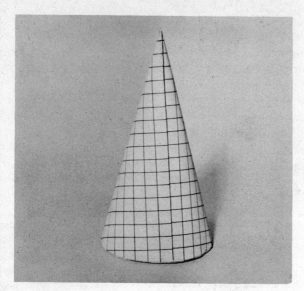

288

289

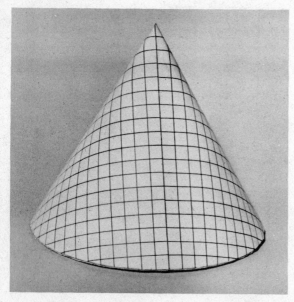

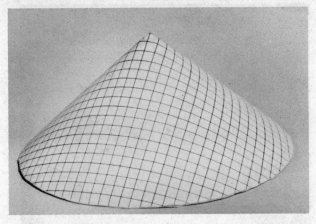

intersects both the others, and through every point of the cone pass lines of two families. We can see from the photographs (**291**, **292**, **293**) how the netlines cross themselves; the vertex of the cones is directed toward the observer.

291

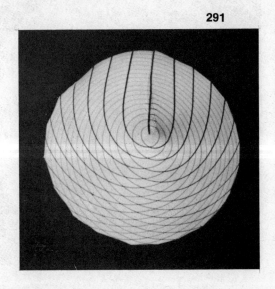

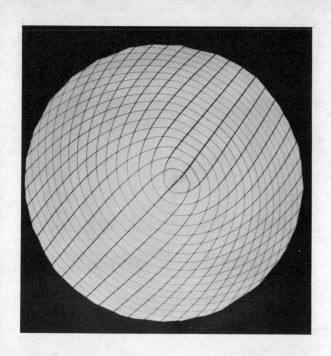

292

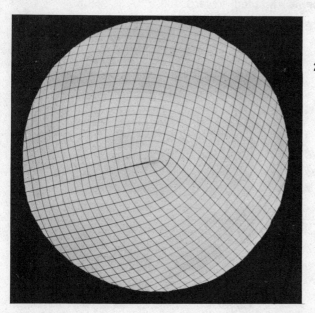

293

10

Squirrels, Screws, Candles, Tunes, and Shadows

It is amusing to watch squirrels running after each other round a tree; their paths are helices. In fact, to find the shortest path on a cylinder, we can cut it along a straight line (**294**) and lay it out flat (as in the map **284**). The shortest route between any two points will give on the picture a straight line; this line, when rolled up back together with the cylinder, changes into a helix (**295**). The projection of a screw (**296**) shows cusps at certain points. It is a property of every skew line that we may obtain from any of its points (**297**) such cusps by an appropriate projection. An ordinary screw has a helix as its edge line. The so-called 'endless' screw (**298**) changes uniform rotating motion into a uniform progressive motion. If a segment of a given length glides with one end on

294

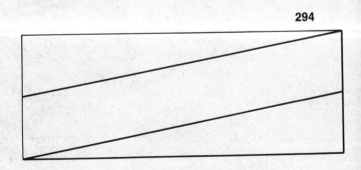

295

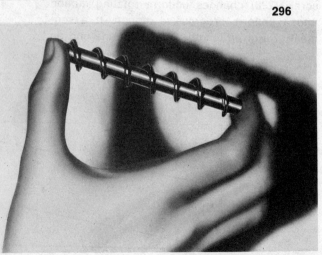

296

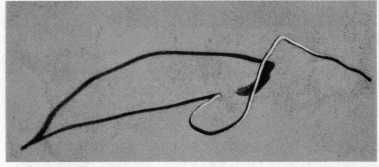

297

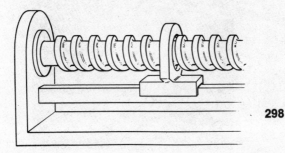

298

a helix, its other end gliding along the axis, a helicoidal (**299**) surface arises. This surface can be obtained by uniformly turning an arm round a rod and by moving the rod uniformly in its own direction at the same time. This surface is the only non-rotary surface capable of gliding on itself. The sphere, the cylinder, and the plane are rotary surfaces; not only can they glide on themselves but they may be so slid over themselves that an arbitrary point will travel on any given track. Hence these four surfaces will always play a dominant part in the structure of machines.

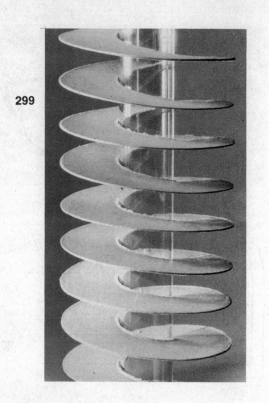

299

300

When we cut a cylinder by a plane, we get an ellipse (**300**). It would be erroneous to consider the ellipse a shortest path on the cylinder because of its lying in one plane. If we wind paper round a candle (**301**), then cut it obliquely (**302**) with a sharp knife (**303**), and then unwind the paper (**304**), we obtain a sinusoid. By adding sinusoids, we can obtain any curve. The lines drawn on the cylinder of a gramophone by the needle when recording a pure note become sinusoids when laid out

301

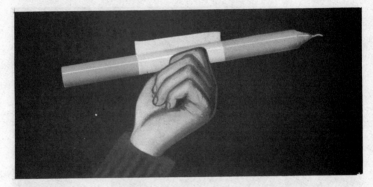

302

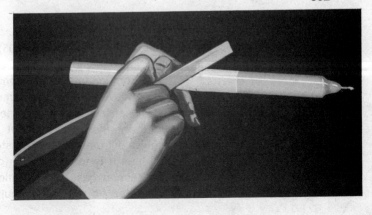

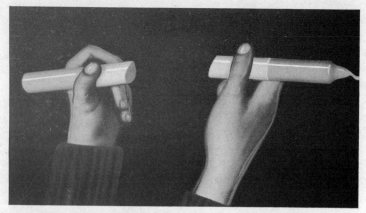

303

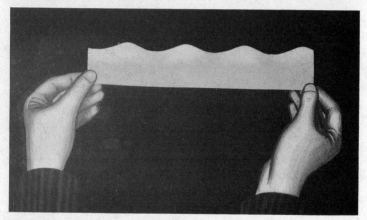

304

flat. Here are three sinusoids **(305)** of equal amplitudes, i.e. equally high; they correspond to the three components of the concord high-C:G:C. The heavy line is the sum of three sinusoids; it is the curve recorded on the gramophone by the concord. But the same concord gives in different circumstances another **(306)** line. It is to be seen on our sketch that in the second case the vibrations of the component notes do not start simultaneously.

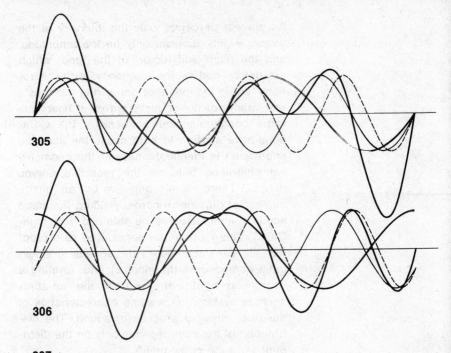

305

306

307

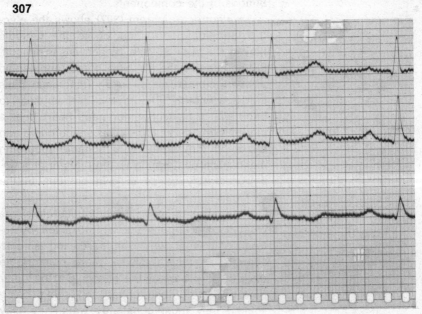

As our ear perceives only the intensity of the sound, which depends only on the amplitude, and the pitch and 'color' of the tune, which are determined by the frequency of the vibrations, but is incapable of perceiving the crests and valleys of the acoustic waves, it hears the same continuous sound whenever the vibrations have started. In both cases the acoustic impression is identical whatever the geometrical difference between the recorded curves may be. There are not only two but an infinite number of different records, yielding the same acoustic impression, to be obtained from high-C:G:C. This fact can be considered as a proof that our ear decomposes the sounds in sinusoidal components (harmonics) and, forming a compound again of them in the cerebronervous system, loses some characteristics of the true, physical process of sound. The distribution of the sum depends only on the distributions of the components.

An electrocardiogram (**307**) shows the electric vibrations corresponding to the periodic play of the heart muscle. Its analysis is difficult. Let us imagine the electrical force represented at every moment as an arrow (mathematicians call it a vector). The arrows placed front to back will circumscribe for each heart beat a closed skew curve (**308**). This space curve can be drawn on paper by a suitable recording mechanism conforming to the rules of descriptive geometry so as to give an idea of the real curve.

When strolling along a sandy beach in shoes most people choose the wet strip left by retreating waves, which is hard and smooth enough to make the walk more comfortable than the dry part of the beach. On the other hand, to avoid their shoes and socks being soaked they must constantly watch the play

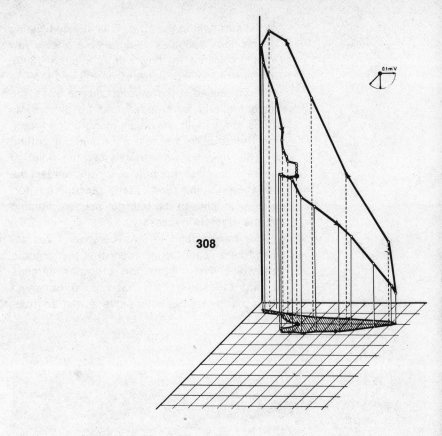

308

309

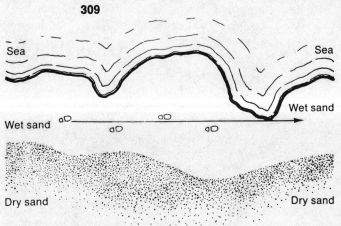

Sea

Sea

Wet sand

Wet sand

Dry sand

Dry sand

of the surf licking the strip. This steady twisting of the neck becomes disagreeable after a few minutes. There is, however, a remedy (**309**). Instead of looking sidewise one keeps looking straight ahead; in every instant he sees the instantaneous water edge and he directs his steps tangentially: he walks along a line touching the edge in a single point without cutting it. This direction is variable but the point of contact lies far enough away to render the variations small and easily accounted for: neither looking to the left, nor sudden jumping to the right is necessary.

The background for the behavior I recommend here (after having tried it) is the 'ergodic principle': The distribution of water tongues licking the shore in a fixed point observed during a long time is the same as the distribu-

310

tions shown in a fixed moment by a long portion of the water edge—the principle involved is the identity of time-distribution and space-distribution. To apply it here the walker has to limit his observation to the part of the shore he will cover in the next minute—in most cases such tactics keep him on the safe side without leading him out of the wet strip of the beach.

All the three familiar curves—ellipse, hyperbola, and parabola—can be got by cutting a cone with a plane in an appropriate manner. They can be obtained consequently as shadows of a circular disc. When we place the disc so that the whole shadow is on the wall, we get an ellipse (**310**); when a part of it casts no shadow on the wall, it is a hyperbola (**311**); (when only a point is situated so as to give no shadow, it is a parabola) (**312**). A ball lying on the table and illuminated from above casts an elliptic shadow and it touches the table at the focus of the ellipse.

The planets wander in ellipses. The sun is one of the foci; the radius sun-planet covers the same area (**313**) every day (every hour, too) but, as the sketch indicates, the earth does not cover the same distance every month.

An elliptical billiard table (**314**) gives for a ball started so as not to pass between the foci a broken course and all the parts of it are tangents to a smaller ellipse with the same foci. If the initial stroke drives the ball between the foci (**315**), it will pass again between them after rebounding from the boundary. Thus it will forever do so; its path will consist of tangents to a hyperbola with the same foci as the table. If the ball starts at a focus, after hitting the boundary (**316**) it passes through the other focus; its course approaches the major axis very closely after a few rebounds.

311

312

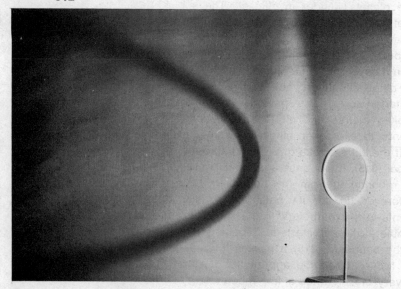

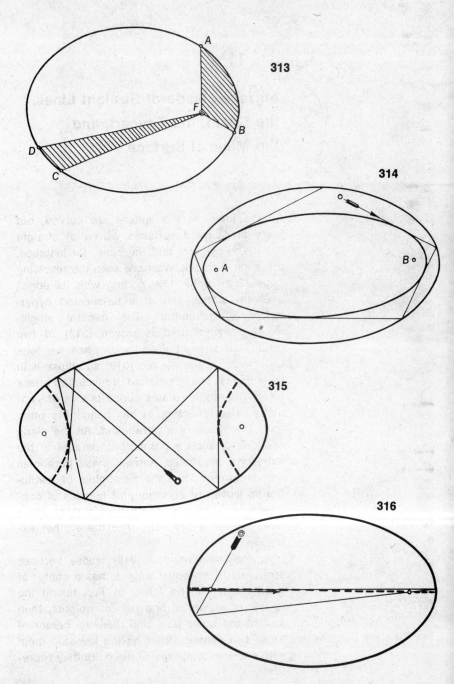

313

314

315

316

11

Surfaces Made of Straight Lines, the Chain, the Toycart, and the Minimal Surface

All the lines on the sphere are curved, but there are curved surfaces woven of straight lines. The cylinder and the cone, for instance, are such surfaces. We have seen the revolving cube (**202**), page 172, gliding with its edges over two cones and a single-sheeted hyperboloid of revolution. The general single-sheeted hyperboloid is woven (**317**) of two groups of straight lines, and, when we look on it from above, we see (**318**) an ellipse with its tangents. The paraboloid of revolution arises when a parabola rotates about its axis of symmetry. The reflectors of car headlights often have the shape of a paraboloid. All the plane sections of such a paraboloid, parallel to the axis, give parabolas, and all these parabolas are congruent. Thus the paraboloid of revolution is woven of an infinity of families of congruent plane curves. The sphere and the plane have the same property. (Are there other examples?)

A skew quadrilateral (**319**) whose vertices are loaded with equal weights has a center of gravity that can be found by first taking the center of gravity of one pair of weights, then that of the other pair, and then the center of these two centers (after having invested them with the united masses of the pairs they repre-

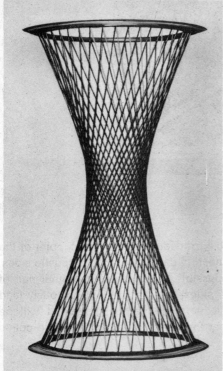

317

318

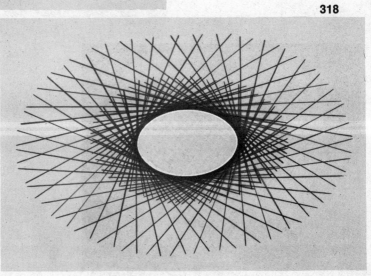

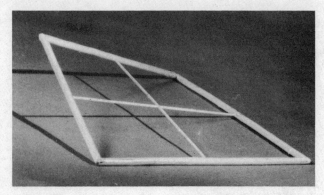

319

sent). This procedure gives the midpoint of the line connecting the midpoints of opposite sides. As it is possible to begin with the other pair of opposite sides, and as this will obviously lead us to the same center of gravity, it will be found that the lines connecting the mid-points

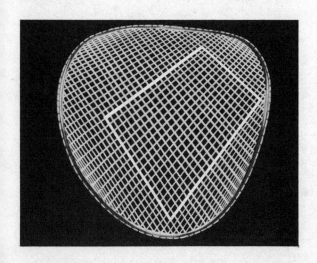

of opposite sides of a skew quadrilateral intersect (and halve) each other. If the weights are
unequal (e.g. *a, b, c, d*) but proportional
($a : b = c : d$), we get lines dividing one pair
of opposite sides in the ratio $a : b$ and the other
in the ratio $b : d$. These lines also intersect
each other, as can be verified by the same
argument. Now we can change the weights
a, b, c, d but retain the proportionality; we
obtain two groups of lines, which form a doubly
woven surface (**320**) on the frame of the quadrilateral (the photograph shows a metal rim
that is not of any significance; we must choose
four threads on the model to have the skew
quadrilateral). Seen from the side, this surface
looks (**321**) like a saddle; it is called a hyperbolic paraboloid.

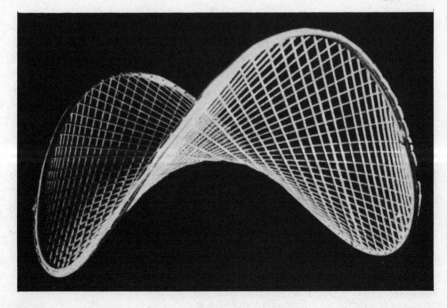

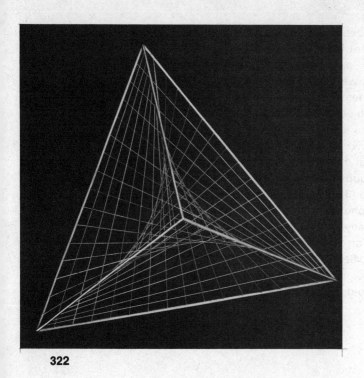

322

Sketch (**322**) shows six equal rods which could serve as a model of a regular tetrahedron with transparent faces. Each rod is divided into 16 equal segments by 15 nodes, a node being the point where a thread is attached. The model consists of three pairs of opposite rods, each rod connected with its opposite by 15 threads. The reader may imagine a thousand nodes instead of fifteen; the resulting tissue of three thousand threads would divide the tetrahedron into eight parts, four of them open and four closed; the reader may compare the volumes of the parts with the tetrahedron's volume. He is warned that the quadrangular lattice (**323**) is an optical illusion, unlike that of photos (**320, 321**), where it is real.

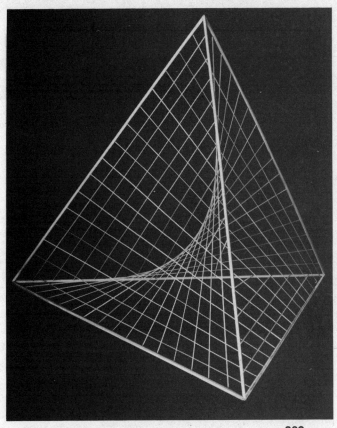

A simple method to get a surface with a
family of straight lines on it is to take a plane
wire with rods tangentially attached to it and
twist it to make a skew curve. We obtain a
double-sheeted surface (**324**) woven of a single
group of straight lines; the curve is a sharp
edge connecting the two sheets and no sheet
extends beyond this edge. If we take two rings
of wire with the same axis (hence placed like
the upper and lower bases of a truncated

324

cone) and dip them into soap suds, there will arise a surface of revolution (**325**), the smallest of all those that may be stretched upon such a fixed frame, because a soap film makes itself as small as possible. The photograph shows both the actual surface itself and its shadow projected on a screen. Its parallels of latitude are circles; its meridian, which is distinctly visible as the upper contour of the shadow on

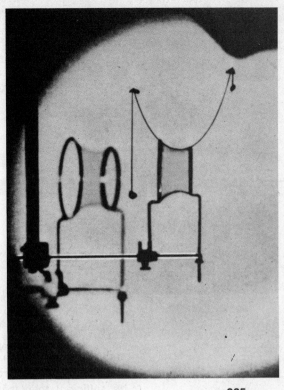

325

the screen, can be enlarged by means of a projector. Then we can take its photograph together with a chain hanging on the screen, and we see that it is distinctly a catenary in form, that is, it has the appearance of a chain hanging between two nails (**326**). The equation of the catenary is $y = a(b^x + b^{-x})$; with appropriate units for x and y, it is $y = 10^x + 10^{-x}$.

To return to the minimal surface of soap suds, we have only to rotate the catenary round its x axis. Now, if the chain is given, we do not see any axis. To find it we have to cut the chain at its lowest point and straighten

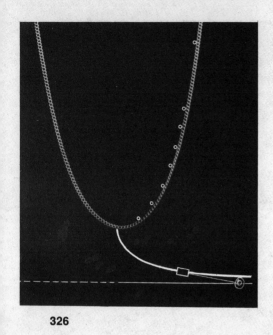

326

it. Let us imagine the chain hanging on a wall and a set of nails on the concave side of the chain preventing it from going back; it would be sufficient then to let the chain fall by the action of gravity. The cut end of the chain would trace the same path as the toy cart (**327**)

327

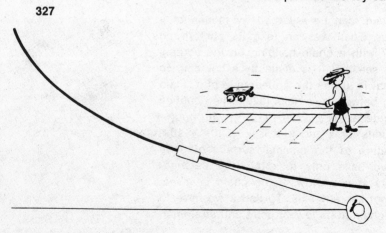

of a child walking along the curbstone and dragging the cart in the street behind. The sidewalk will never be reached by the cart, which approaches it more and more; the curb is the axis sought for. Thus we find it as the highest of all horizontal lines that cannot be touched by the end of the chain cut at its lowest point and allowed to fall freely down.

The tractrix traced by the toy (or the developed chain) can be turned about the child's route as axis (i.e. about the same axis as that found for the catenoid) to give a new surface of revolution, which has the property that a flexible lamina fitted to it can be moved all over its surface, bending without stretching, always fitting the surface, and never crumpling. The same property is shared by the sphere, the cylinder, the cone, the plane, and by all surfaces got by folding the plane. Our surface has, however, the peculiarity of negative curvature; every point of it is a saddle point. This curvature is everywhere constant, as on the sphere; this we can see by sliding the lamina along itself. This is also the reason why the tractrisoid is sometimes called a pseudo-sphere or also an antisphere.

12

Platonic Bodies Again, Crossing Bridges, Tying Knots, Coloring Maps, and Combing Hair

We have stated previously that there are only five regular polyhedra, the so-called five Platonic bodies, without giving any reason why this is so. Let us draw on a sphere a figure having L lines, V vertices, and F faces; in other words, let us divide the globe into F countries (we shall consider seas and oceans as land). Then we shall have $V + F = L + 2$, whatever the political situation may be. It is not difficult to verify this rule, discovered by Euler, the great Swiss mathematician. Let us start with

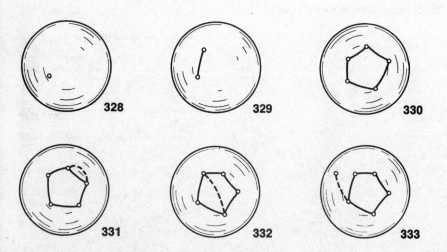

328   329   330

331   332   333

one vertex (**328**); taking the rule to the letter, we see its truth in this case, because there is one vertex ($V = 1$), one face ($F = 1$), and no lines ($L = 0$): $1 + 1 = 0 + 2$. Drawing one line from the vertex (**329**), we get a new division of the sphere and the rule obviously holds, as we have $V = 2$, $F = 1$, and $L = 1$ ($2 + 1 = 1 + 2$). Now let us suppose we had any figure with the rule holding (**330**) and let us draw a new line connecting (**331**), (**332**) a vertex to another already existing vertex. We thus increase the number of vertices by 0, the number of faces by 1, and the number of lines by 1; this step means increasing by 1 the left and the right side of Euler's rule and it would obviously hold for the new division if it held before. If the new line ends with a new vertex (**333**), the increase in the number of vertices is 1, that of faces 0, and that of lines 1; the argument applies again. As we can draw any figure on the sphere, beginning with a vertex and then tracing the necessary lines one after another, Euler's rule is established. (What is the connection with dominoes?) Among all possible divisions of the sphere the regular ones in which we are interested are characterized by having the same number f of lines as a boundary of every face and the same number v of lines meeting at every vertex. If there are F faces, the product Ff gives the total number of lines, each line being counted twice, because each line belongs to two faces. Thus $2L = Ff$. We can also count the lines vertex by vertex; this gives $2L = Vv$. Thus we get

$$F = 2L/f, \quad V = 2L/v;$$

replacing V and F in Euler's rule by the fractions found here, we get

$$2L/v + 2L/f = L + 2,$$

which can be written also as

(E) $1/v + 1/f = 1/L + 1/2.$

The easiest way to satisfy this equation is to put either

$f = 2, v = L$ or $v = 2, f = L.$

The first assumption gives $F = L, V = 2$. So we have only two vertices and as many faces as lines; as $v = L$, every line belongs to every vertex, and as $f = 2$, every face is bounded by two lines. Thus we have two poles (**334**) joined by L meridians; the number of meridians is arbitrary ($L = 1, 2, 3, \ldots$). The second assumption gives $V = L, F = 2$. Now we have only two faces and as many vertices as lines; as $f = L$, every line belongs to every face, i.e. the common boundary of the two faces is composed of L lines and L vertices. Thus we have the globe (**335**) divided in two hemispheres separated by an L-gon; the number L is arbitrary. We shall call these two kinds of maps exceptional; let us remark that the case $f = 2$, $v = 2$ belongs to both of them (**336**).

Returning to the general equation (E), let us try $L = 1$; we can see easily that the only solutions we get are the exceptional ones, $v = 1, f = 2$ (a closed line with one vertex on it), or $v = 2, f = 1$, already found (**329**). The same thing applies to $L = 2$, which gives only the solution $f = v = 2$ mentioned above.

334

335

336

Thus to get new divisions of the sphere we must assume $L = 3, 4, 5, \ldots$ The right side of (E) then becomes less than 1 and, as it is always greater than 1/2, we have

$$1/2 < 1/f + 1/v < 1$$

The value $f = 1$ is incompatible with the right-hand inequality and the value $f = 2$ gives the exceptional case of (**334**), already dealt with. Let us begin then with $f = 3$. We can try here only $v = 3, 4$, and 5, because $v = 1$ is incompatible with the right inequality, $v = 2$ gives a case dealt with before, and $v = 6$ or more gives for the sum $1/f + 1/v = 1/3 + 1/v$ the value 1/2 or less, contrary to the left inequality. The same argument shows that putting f greater than 3, we are limited to $v = 3, 4, 5$, by the left inequality. As we can begin with v (which must be 3 at least, if we are to avoid impossible or exceptional cases), we see that f is limited to 3, 4, and 5. We have consequently $3 \times 3 = 9$ cases combining the two sets 3, 4, 5. Four of them,

$$f = 4, v = 4; \qquad f = 4, v = 5;$$
$$f = 5, v = 4; \qquad f = 5, v = 5;$$

are impossible because of the left inequality: $1/4 + 1/4 = 1/2$ is already too small. Five cases are left:

(a) $f = 3, v = 3$, (E) gives here
$1/3 + 1/3 - 1/2 = 1/L, L = 6, F = 4, V = 4$

(b) $f = 3, v = 4$; (E) gives here
$1/3 + 1/4 - 1/2 = 1/L, L = 12, F = 8, V = 6$

(c) $f = 3, v = 5$; (E) gives here
$L = 30, F = 20, V = 12$

(d) $f = 4, v = 3$; (E) gives here
$L = 12, F = 6, V = 8$

(e) $f = 5, v = 3$; (E) gives here
$L = 30, F = 12, V = 20.$

We have finally found the five regular divisions of the sphere. The exceptional solutions yield no polyhedra in the usual sense, because we have neither two-sided polygons with straight sides nor two-faced polyhedra with plane faces. The five Platonic bodies corresponding to (a), (b), (c), (d), and (e) are the only regular polyhedra: tetrahedron, octahedron, icosahedron, cube, and dodecahedron.

Let us realize that we have proved much more than we promised. We have found all regular maps on the globe whatever the frontiers may be, without any assumptions in regard to their being circles or tortuous lines. Moreover, the exact shape of the globe is immaterial for our statements, which hold as well for a cube- or a lens-shaped planet as for a spherical one.

Such things are similar to the old problem of drawing figures without lifting the pencil and passing once and only once through each point. This is possible for the drawing (337). Euler came across the question of what figures can be so drawn when he was set the problem of the Königsberg bridges (338). There are seven of them, and the question is this: is it

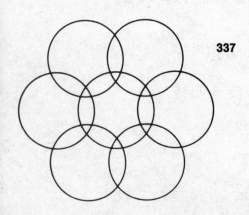

337

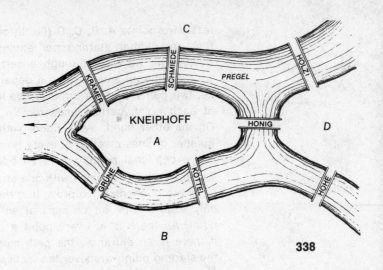

338

possible to cross them all in turn, passing no more than once over each? If we indicate the island by *A*, the left bank of the river by *B*, the right one by *C*, and the area between the two arms of the upper course by *D*, our task will consist in drawing, with one stroke of the pencil, a certain figure (**339**) consisting of seven lines. The task is, however, impossible, for having chosen any given point as the point of departure and any other as the goal, we should have to pass, on the way, through at

339

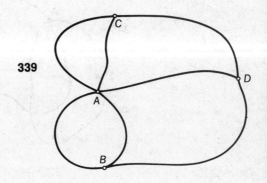

least two points A, B, C, D (i.e. through those that are neither starting nor ending points). Every time we pass through a certain point, we describe an entering and a departing path, i.e. two paths, and, as three or five lines meet at each point, certain lines remain undrawn. On the other hand, every figure with an even number of lines meeting at every point, or with two exceptional points where an odd number is allowed, can be drawn with one stroke, if its parts are connected. To prove it in the case of only even points, let us start at an arbitrary point. As there is at every point a departure if there is an entrance, the path must end at the starting point, whatever the tactics we have chosen. We can consider the whole path as a closed curve; if there remain parts of the figure not already visited, they must be linked with the paths in one of its points A; of the paths leading to A, an even number belong to the old path and an even number to the other parts. Now let us travel round the closed curve beginning at A and finishing at A (**340**). As A belongs to the other part too, we can choose it now for a starting point and draw a new,

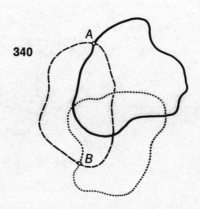

340

closed curve from *A* to *A*. It is easy to see that two closed curves with a common point *A* can be considered as one closed curve (as the figure 8 is one). If our task is not yet accomplished, this new closed curve must be linked at *B* with the rest of the figure; this reasoning can be applied anew and leads finally to the solution. The case of two exceptional points of odd order is to be treated similarly. We have only to start at an exceptional point *O*; it is obvious that whatever way we choose, it will end at the other point of odd order *O'*. The rest of the figure has no exceptional points; it is therefore a closed curve linked at a certain point *B* (341) with the first path *O*—*O'*. Now we can start at *O*, go on the path *O*—*O'* to *B*, travel round the closed curve back to *B*, and finish the journey by *B*—*O'* on the first path.

341

What you see on (342) is a white thread wound around 23 nails and showing a polygon of 23 sides with all diagonals. This a proof that this polygon and all starred 23-gons form together a single closed curve. The winding took 45 minutes. The same trick would be impossible for a 24-gon and would take much more time for a 25-gon. (Why?)

Nails excepted, the thread passes through no point more than twice.

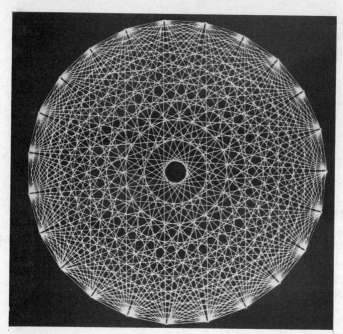

342

Let us look at a closed chain that (**343**) crosses itself once. When we move it on the table so as to let the crossing vanish, we must pass through a stage (**344**) when the chain 'breaks,' i.e. when a sharp point appears. To prove this statement, let us consider the tangent (**345**). Its angle with a fixed direction changes when we travel round the chain, but its increments are cancelled by its decrements, and the total variation during the whole circuit is zero. For a chain without crossing, the total variation is 360°; thus there must be a last shape of the chain with the variation zero; it is just the shape with a sharp point, where the tangent cancels abruptly at one point the variation of its angle acquired during the whole circuit.

343

344

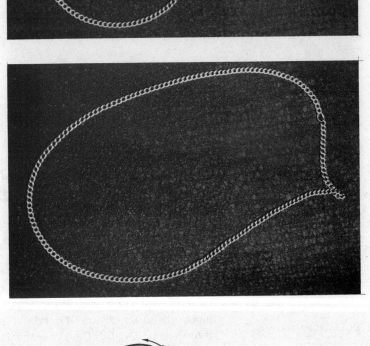

345

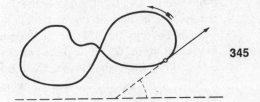

346

The sketch (**346**) illustrates a different problem. Here we have three houses, a dovecot, a well, and a haystack; three paths are to be traced from each house, one to the dovecot, one to the well, and the third to the haystack, but so arranged that they do not intersect each other. The problem proves to be impossible, for, if we connect the first house with the well, the haystack, and the dovecot, and then proceed through these points along the paths connecting them with the second house, we shall have three lines leading from one house to the other (**347**) and never crossing. These lines obviously divide the whole plane into three areas: C_1, C_2, C_3. Now, the third house surely lies in one of them. If it lies in C_1, it will be beyond the closed line including the haystack; if in C_2, it will be within another closed line, while the dovecot will be outside; if in C_3, it will be surrounded by a line beyond which the well lies. In the first case, the hay-

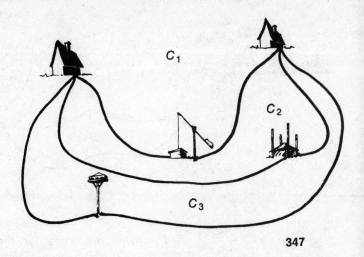

stack will remain unconnected with the house, in the second, with the dovecot, in the third, with the well.

Let us consider four countries, every pair being neighbors. Their capitals can, therefore, be connected by railways, each line running only through the territories of the two terminal stations. Beginning with three capitals A, B, C, we get a sort of triangle. The capital D is interior or exterior to this triangle; joining it by railways to A, B, and C, we get, in both cases, a great triangle composed of three adjacent triangular parts. Now consider the capital E of a fifth country; it (348) must lie either in one of the small triangles or outside the great one. In either case there is one capital X (A, B, C, or D) separated from E by a triangle of railways. Since these lines pass entirely through territories belonging neither to X nor to E, the capital E is no neighbor of X. Thus five countries are never neighbors of each other.

348

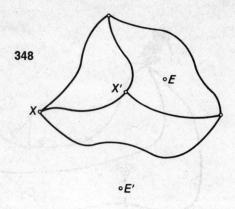

Topology is the name for the chapter of geometry with which we are dealing here, and the science of knots also belongs to it. A cord with its ends connected (**349**) remains unknotted forever, if no knot has been tied on it before splicing. If, however, there initially was a knot (**350**), it never disappears (**351**)

349

350

without cutting the string. The simplest knot can assume two distinct forms (**352**), which cannot be transformed into each other by pulling the string without cutting it; one is a mirror image of the other.

It is possible to shift a knot along a string as far as we like, but it is impossible to tie two knots on two ends of a string in such a manner that when brought together, they may cancel each other. Recently a mathematical proof of this empirical fact has been found.

352

353

354A

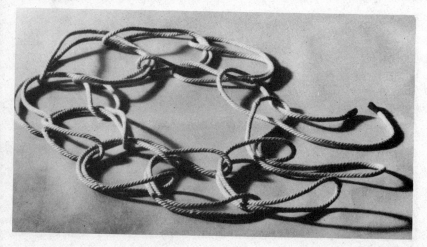

It is easy to make three closed curves interlocked as a whole (**353**) with no pair of them
being interlocked; it can be seen at once that
a cut in any of the strings lets all three fall
asunder. It is even possible to make a model
of any number of closed curves (**354A, B**) with
the same properties.

354 B

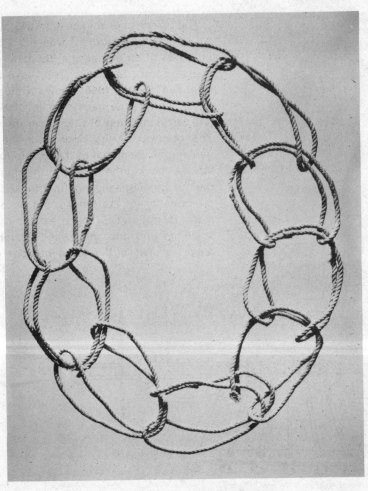

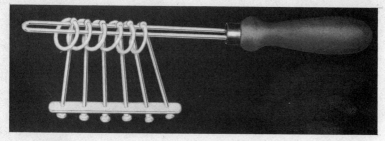

355

The device shown in sketch (**355**), which was called a 'baguenaudier,' was used by French peasants of an earlier age. Its name and practical purpose, to lock chests, have now been forgotten. Sketch (**356**) shows a closed chest: to lift the lid it is necessary to disengage the left part consisting of rings from the right part. The removal of the rings with the iron bar hanging on them makes it possible to open the lock by moving the handle to the right. The left part is topologically not interlocked with the prolongation of the handle, but its disengagement is not easy. There exists, however, a solution; and the interesting feature of the *baguenaudier* is the large number of moves

356

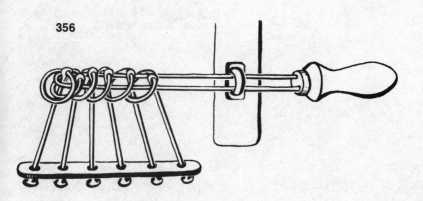

necessary to separate left from right, in spite of the apparent simplicity of the device. With 6 rings it is already a problem; with 12 rings it would take several hundreds of moves. The number of parts is very small when compared with the time required.

357

A strip of paper twisted through an angle of 180° and gummed together (the so-called Möbius band) is a unilateral surface (**357**). A fly can crawl over the whole of it without the inconvenience of crossing its edge. This edge forms one closed, but not knotted, curved line.

The model (**357**) might suggest that the stiffness of twisted paper is an essential feature of the Möbius band, which is not so. To look at it from a better point of view let us consider a model (**358**) where a ribbon is wound on three transparent cylinders; their axes cross at 60° and the silken ribbon can be twisted without resistance but its extensibility is nil. This model shows that people living on a Möbius-band planet could employ a system of parallels and meridians crossing at 90°; their cartographers would be happy: their maps could be

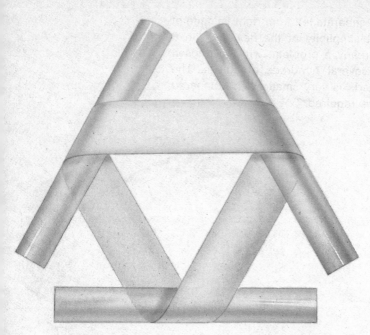

358

flat, lengths of curves on them would be proportional to true lengths, angles on maps equal to real angles, and areas on maps proportional to areas on the planet.

If we cut the Möbius band along the black line parallel to the edges, it does not fall asunder, but forms a bilateral (**359**) surface. The strip has now two closed curved lines as margins; they are not individually knotted, but interwoven with one another. A simpler band having the same properties (bilateral surface, two interwoven, not knotted margins) can easily be obtained (**360**) by twisting a paper ribbon to an angle of 360° before gumming it, while the first band is twisted to 720°. There is another surface of exactly the same properties as the band of (**360**); this is its image in the

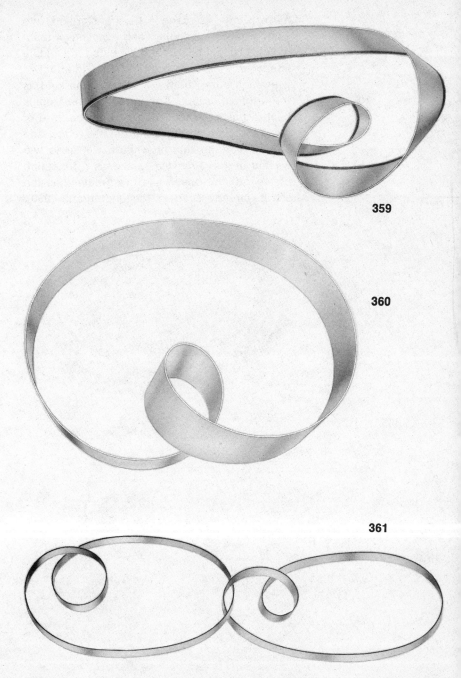

359

360

361

271

mirror; the two cannot be transformed into each other by bending and twisting without cutting. The surface, when cut along the middle line gives rise to two strips (**361**) interlocked with each other; both are of the same kind as the original surface. Tracing along the Möbius band a black line at a distance of one-third of the band's breadth (**362**) from the edge and cutting it along this line, there will arise two twisted strips (**363**); the smaller is a repetition of the original one, while the greater has the shape already seen in the photograph (**360**).

362

363

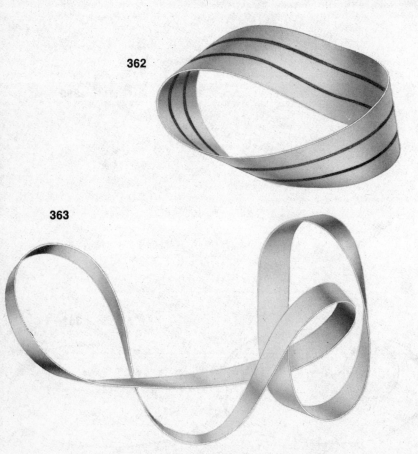

If we twist the ribbon to the extent of three semi-revolutions, that is, to 540°, before gumming, the result will again be a unilateral surface (**364**), the edge of which will be one knotted curve, the knot being of the kind seen on the left side of (**352**), page 265. An ordinary sheet, a leaf for instance, is two-sided, its edge unknotted. Hence arises the question: does there exist a bilateral surface with a knotted edge? A positive answer to this query is the model beneath (**365**). The edge is again a knot like the one on the left side of (**352**).

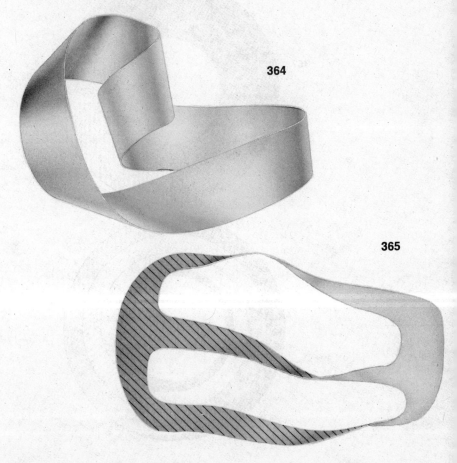

364

365

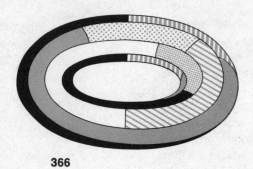

366

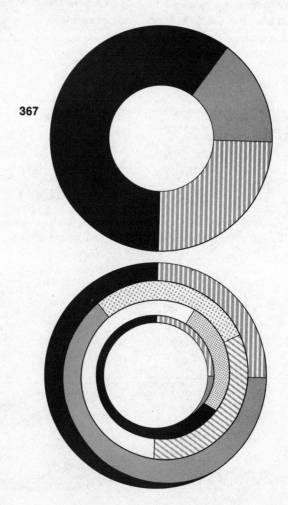

367

274

It is well known that one can color any map drawn on a sphere or a plane in four hues, so that the neighboring countries are distinguishable from each other by their different colors. This fact has not been proved rigorously, but experiment has shown it to be so. For a torus (**366**), i.e. a surface in the form of a pneumatic tire, we should require as many as seven colors, for it is possible to draw a map on it showing seven countries, each of them contiguous with all others. The views of the torus from above and from beneath (**367**) give the disposition of the seven countries.

Although the torus is a less trivial surface than the plane or the sphere, it has been rigorously proved that on it seven colors are always sufficient. So far only the sufficiency of *five* colors on the plane or sphere has been demonstrated but no example is known in which the fifth color would be necessary.

It is possible to draw on the torus a closed line that does not cross itself and is identical with the left-hand knot on page 265 (**368**). By cutting the torus along the black line, i.e. along

368

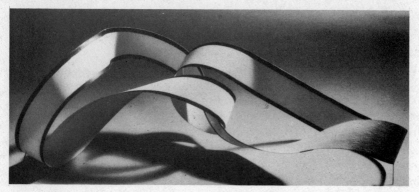

369

the knot, we get a bilateral surface (**369**) with
two edges; they are interlocked and both of
them are knots of the same kind as the original
one. To build it up directly, we must twist a
strip by three full revolutions (1080°) and knot
it before gumming. A bilateral surface limited
by two knotted but not interlocked edges is
obtained by a junction (**370**) of two models of a
previously described shape.

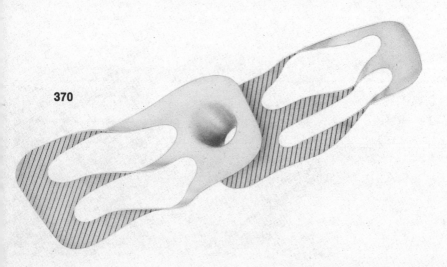

370

It is possible (**371**) to place on the torus any number of knots of the left-hand type in (**352**) with no one of them cutting itself or any other. If, however, we place both knots of (**352**) on a torus, they will produce 12 intersections (**372**).

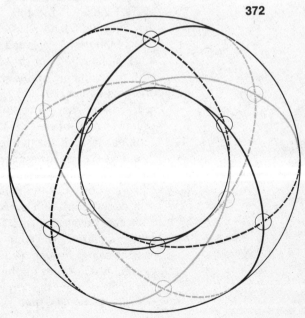

372

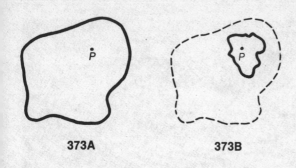

373A   **373B**

If a flat region of any kind (**373A**) made of an elastic material contracts so as to occupy finally only a part (**373B**) of the area it originally covered, there will be always a point (*P*) that occupies the same place after contraction as before. The proof, based on the property (**32–33**) of chessboards, uses an idea of W. Stozek. We consider the chessboard as the given region and *Q* as the position of point *P* after contraction. We call a square red, if for every *P* belonging to this square *Q* lies nearer the right side than *P*, green if the foregoing holds with 'right' replaced by 'left,' and yellow if it is neither red nor green. It is easy to verify that the squares of the left column are not green and those of the right column are not red. It is as easy to verify that red and green squares are never neighbors: neighboring squares have at least one point in common. It follows that yellow squares, if prohibited for the king, prevent his traveling from the left to the right border of the chessboard; and hence —in accordance with property (**32–33**)—that a rook can travel from top to bottom along the yellow squares. Thus one could draw a line passing only through yellow squares, joining the upper edge with the base. In each point of this line we draw the arrow *PQ*. Not all those arrows can be directed upward (i.e. not all *Q* can lie higher than P), because the point P cannot pass to a point Q beyond the chessboard. The same reasoning yields that not all arrows can be directed downward. The direction of arrows alters continuously along this line, thus the line contains at least one point P' with a horizontal $P'Q'$. We conclude from the definition of the yellow square containing P', that there exists also a point P'' with a vertical $P''Q''$, for otherwise all the arrows PQ for this square would face the same direction (left or right) as $P'Q'$ and the square would be colored red or green. If the square is small, such an abrupt change of direction is impossible unless the arrow PQ is small itself for all P of the square. Let us consider a division of the board into n^2 squares, and let n increase; we reach in the limit a point P_0 with vanishing P_0Q_0 *(i.e. $P_0 \equiv Q_0$)*—which means that the contraction does not alter the position of P_0.

If a sphere made of an elastic tissue is folded and distorted (but not torn) so as to become flat, there are necessarily two antipodes, A and B, which come to lie one upon another in the new situation (**374A, B**). There is a curious consequence of this theorem: at

374A

374B

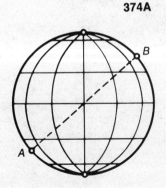

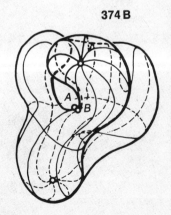

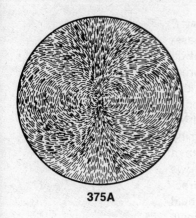

375A

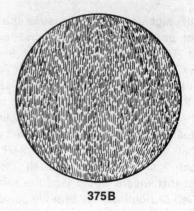

375B

376

every time there is on our globe a pair of antipodes having both the same temperature and the same air pressure. A hairy sphere cannot be combed smoothly as a whole; there is always at least one whirlpoint (**375A, B**) where the hair has no definite direction.

There is no topological difference between the surface of a giraffe's body and that of a zebra. Thus the problem of painting white stripes on the surfaces is in both cases the same; nevertheless nature has found different solutions (**376, 377**).

377

13

Board of Fortune, Frogs, Freshmen, and Sunflowers

The laws of nature lead to various curves. On the diagram (**378**) the curved lines show the connection between the pressure *P* and the volume *V* of one kilogram of gas. The heavy lines are isotherms, i.e. lines of the same temperature. According to the law of Boyle

378

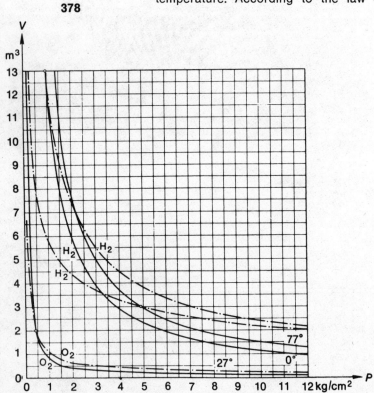

and Mariotte, they are hyperbolas. Hydrogen (H_2) is represented by two isotherms, one for 0°, the other for 77°. The law of Boyle and Mariotte is $PV =$ constant. The dotted lines appear when at a certain moment (the point indicated on the diagram by a small circle) the vessel is surrounded by a coating impervious to heat. The temperature then changes in accordance with the decrease or increase of pressure and we obtain adiabatic lines: they are generalized hyperbolas ($P^a \cdot V^b = k$, a constant). If we plot P and V on logarithmic scales (see (**101**), page 91), all the lines (**379**) become straight.

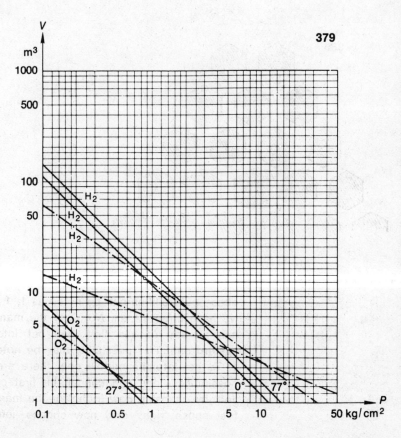

The following picture (**380**) shows a system of islets with channels leading between them. We can imagine it to be a plan of a town. People coming in hesitate at every bifurcation, trying to decide whether they are to choose the left or the right street. There is first only one street downtown and therefore no choice. As to the two following streets in the direction *NS*, a person gets into the western one by avoiding the first street to the left; by avoiding it to the right, he gets into the eastern street.

380

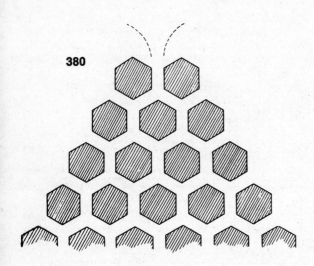

These possibilities can be noted as 1, 1. Next we have three streets *NS*. Only the man who has already chosen 'left' can get into the eastern one. This possibility may be noted by 1. To get into the middle one, there are two possibilities: one can cancel the first choice 'left' by choosing now 'right,' or the man who first chose 'right' may now choose 'left.' As

to the western street, there is only one possible way to get there. These possibilities may
be noted as 1, 2, 1. By adding the neighboring
numbers, we get from 1, 2, 1 the set 1, 3, 3, 1,
which obviously represents all possibilities for
the next four streets. By proceeding in this
manner, we obtain Pascal's triangle:

$$
\begin{array}{ccccccccccc}
& & & & & 1 & & & & & \\
& & & & 1 & & 1 & & & & \\
& & & 1 & & 2 & & 1 & & & \\
& & 1 & & 3 & & 3 & & 1 & & \\
& 1 & & 4 & & 6 & & 4 & & 1 & \\
1 & & 5 & & 10 & & 10 & & 5 & & 1 \\
\end{array}
$$

<pre>
                1
              1   1
            1   2   1
          1   3   3   1
        1   4   6   4   1
      1   5 10 10   5   1
    1   6 15 20 15   6   1
  1   7 21 35 35 21   7   1
1   8 28 56 70 56 28   8   1
1 9 36 84 126 126 84 36   9   1
</pre>

The last line on the diagram represents in how
many ways the people can reach the first, the
second . . . the tenth street of the tenth row.
The total number of possibilities for this row
is $1 + 9 + 36 + 84 + 126 + 126 + 84 +$
$+ 36 + 9 + 1 = 512 = 2^9$. In anthropology,
the human stature, for instance, may be considered a result of many causes acting in the
course of its development, some of which tend
to lower the stature, others to increase it. We
can imagine every individual choosing by toss-
ing a coin whether he takes from nature an
inch more to his stature or gives away from
what he has got already. If he is allowed to do
it nine times and if there are 512 people doing
the same, we can guess by analogy with the
people walking through the town what will
probably happen. We can consider each loss
of an inch as a decision to go right, each

gain as a decision to go left. As there are 512 people, we can exhaust all possibilities written in the last line of Pascal's triangle. If they all occur, we shall have 1 man five inches short of the average stature, 9 men four inches shorter than the average, 36 men three inches shorter, . . . , 126 men one inch over the average, 84 men two inches over the average, . . . , 1 man five inches over the average stature. If we place them so that the tallest stand in the foremost rank, those shorter by an inch in the second rank, and so on, we shall have ten ranks, and the right wing of the squad will form a curve determined by Pascal's numbers, provided that the left one has been arranged as a straight line. We can get this curve of Gauss in several ways. First we can draw it, taking Pascal's numbers as ordinates. Then we can assemble, for instance, all Princeton freshmen of a year and place them in ranks according to their stature (**381**). Finally,

381

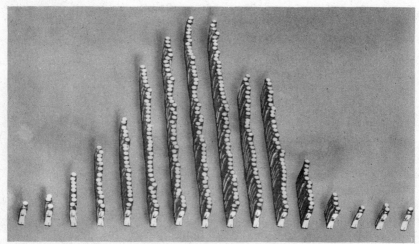

we can make a wooden 'board of fortune' (**382**) with hexagonal islets and channels between them. By inclining the board and pouring small beads into the funnel at the top, we could catch them in boxes beneath the last row of channels and verify the Gauss law of chance by determining whether the columns of beads in actual tests are more or less proportionate to Pascal's numbers. We can simplify the last experiment by employing a board without islets (**383, 384**); we only pour beads from one point and catch them in boxes. This procedure corresponds to an infinity of infinitely small islets;

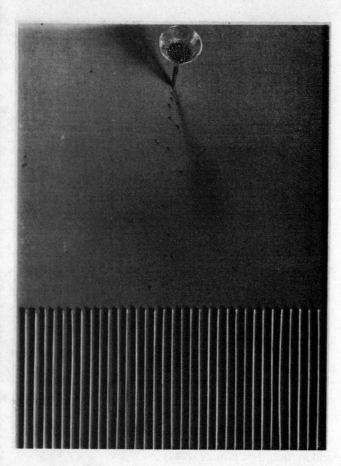

383

the exact Gauss law, of which Pascal's triangle gives only an approximation, has been established mathematically only for an infinity of infinitely small causes working independently; thus an ordinary board without islets serves our purpose better.

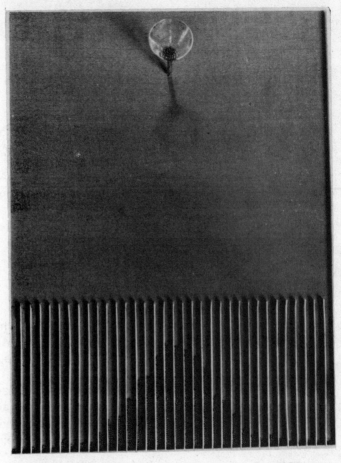

384

Trevan's experiments on the action of digitalis on a frog showed that of a hundred frogs subjected to the injections of digitalis, in quantities indicated on the horizontal (logarithmic) scale (dose for each 10 decagrams of the frog's weight), as many die as are to be found

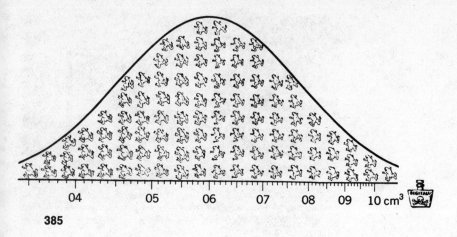

385

on the sketch to the left of the vertical line (**385**) defined by that dose. An injection of 0.4 cc (per 100 g), for instance, will suffice in 6 cases, while one of 0.6 cc, will kill in 50 cases. (How much is necessary to kill 100 frogs?) Of course, these are average figures of many tests. The curve of the 'frog line' is, in this case also, Gauss's curve; its equation is

$$y = A \cdot 10^{c(x-b)^2} \quad (c \text{ is negative}).$$

In matters connected with the development of organisms within a limited space, we find another type of curve. Thornton discovered that bacteria kept in a closed vessel increase to a population depending upon the volume they occupy—in a manner perfectly similar (**386**) to that of sunflowers with regard to the average height (as shown by experiments of Reed and Holland) (**387**), or to that of the American rail-

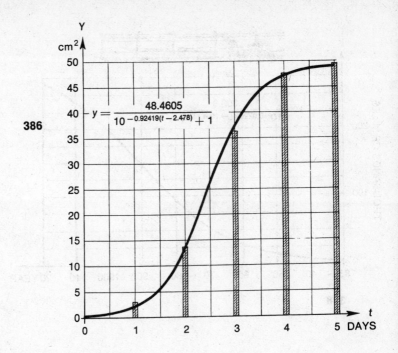

386

$$y = \frac{48.4605}{10^{-0.92419(t - 2.478)} + 1}$$

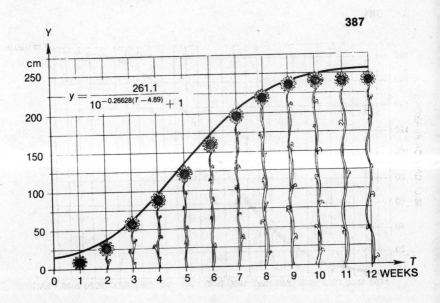

387

$$y = \frac{261.1}{10^{-0.26628(T - 4.89)} + 1}$$

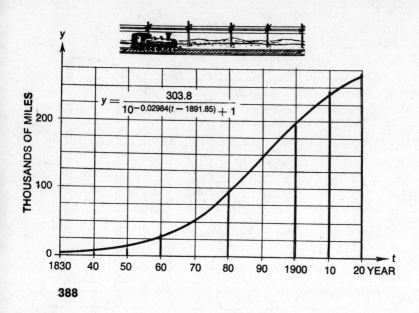

$$y = \frac{303.8}{10^{-0.02984(t - 1891.85)} + 1}$$

388

389

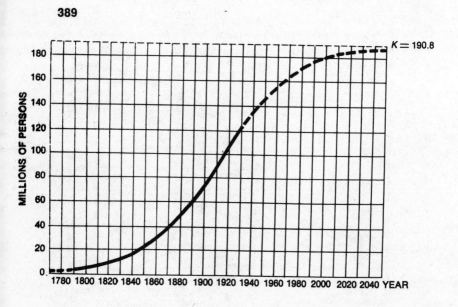

292

ways with regard to the total length (388). The reason for this development is that the increase is proportional to the number of organisms already living, as well as to the (decreasing) space still available. The drawings show also the small discrepancies between the theoretic curve and the real data. The American population exhibits the same law of growth (389); it is given by the equation

$$Y = \frac{190830.35}{1 + 10^{1.542035 - 0.01366265\ (t-1800)}}$$

(t signifies the year, Y the population in thousands). The curve has an inflection; it can be shown that the upper limit, approached by the curve as the time increases indefinitely, lies twice as high as the point of inflection. On this ground statisticians calculated the upper limit of the population of the United States as being 160 millions. Our curve gives around 191 millions. This difference is due to the fact that it is rather difficult to determine the exact position of the point of inflection; the real curve consists of single points which can be joined into a single smooth line in many ways. Whatever one may think of such arguments, it is true that soon after the inflection point was reached, bills were voted to stop immigration; other symptoms could be observed in favor of the thesis that the space available was limited and was already felt as such.

The survey of the last years shows that the growth of the population has overcome the obstacles limiting its size.

We have also a great many other curves in the domain of natural science, though their laws are not based upon theoretical deduction: e.g. the curve showing the distribution

293

(**390**) of land and sea at various altitudes (the horizontal scale indicates that at a depth of 8000 meters there is 100 per cent land, at a depth of 4000 meters only 60 per cent, at sea level approximately 30 per cent and finally at the height of 9000 meters there is 0 per cent land and 100 per cent air). Another example is a graph (**391**) showing the mortality of males in the United States.

390

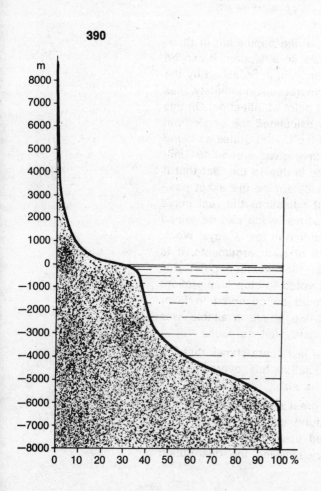

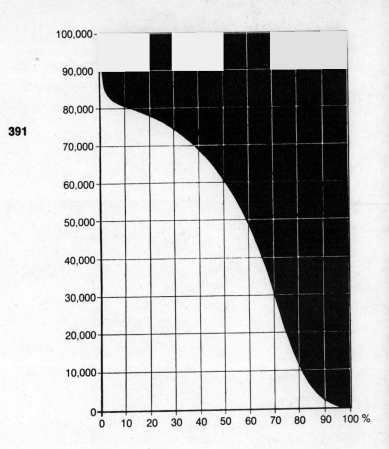

Notes

(The numbers refer to the illustrations or accompanying text.)

(1) H. E. Dudeney, *Amusements in Mathematics,* London, 1917, p. 27.

(3) Pythagoras of Samos (*c.* 582-507 B.C.), the author of the theorem on right triangles, considered the problem of regular tesselations and the theory of musical harmony. The dissection, however, is a Hindu achievement; the original drawing bears the inscription 'Look!' which must convince the reader better than any verbal argument.

(5) This is an idea of Professor J. Mikusiński.

(8) F. Morley, 'On reflexive geometry, *Trans. Amer. Math. Soc.* 8 (1907), pp. 14-24; J. M. Child, 'Proof of Morley's Theorem,' *Math Gazette* 11 (1923), p. 171.

(9) T. Wazewski, in *Ann. de la Soc. Polonaise de Mathématique* 18 (1945), p. 164, quotes a lawyer, Mr. Rappaport, as the author of this trisection. The error is less than $22'$ $23''$; for angles less than 30° it is less than $1'$.

(10) We have not considered the question of *all* the squares being of different sizes; to make it still more difficult we could prescribe a limit not to be surpassed by the size of the squares employed.

(11) This decomposition of the rectangle was given by Z. Moroń, in *Przegląd Mat.-Fiz.* 3 (1925), pp. 152-3.

(12) T. H. Willcocks published this dissection in the *Fairy Chess Review,* Vol. 7 (1948). R. Sprague *Mathematische Zeitschrift* 45 (1939, pp. 607-8) was the first to dissect a square into different squares. He showed how to cut it into 55 squares. The impossibility of dividing a rectangle into less than 9 different squares has been proved by H. Reichard and H. Toepken in *Jahresbericht der Deutschen Math. Vereinigung* 50 (1940), *Aufgaben und Lösungen,* pp. 13-14. See also 'A note on some perfect squared squares' by T. H. Willcocks in the *Canadian Journal of Mathematics* 3 (1951), pp. 304-8.

(13) H. E. Dudeney, op. cit. p. 27. J. G.-Mikusiński, *Ann. Univ. M. Curie-Sklodowska,* 1 (1946), (Section A), pp. 45-50, gives the graphical demonstration (p. 49).

(16) W. Ahrens gives the theory of different games in *Mathematische Unterhaltungen und Spiele,* Leipzig, Teubner, 1910; I, pp. 172-76. *The Theory of Games and Economic Behavior* is the title of a book by J. v. Neumann and O. Morgenstern (2nd edition, Princeton, 1947) in which the theory of games is subjected to a thorough logical and mathematical analysis. This theory is explained in a simpler manner by J. C. C. McKinsey in his *Introduction to the Theory of Games,* New York, McGraw-Hill, 1952.

(17) Dr. J. Berger, *Columbia Chess Chronicle,* 1888. According to the analysis of W. Hetper, the longest defense of Black is the following one:

White	Black	White	Black
1. $Q-QKt8$	$B-QB5$	8. $K-Kt3$	$B-Kt3$
2. $Q-K5$	$B-QR3$	9. $Q-QB1$	$B-KR4$
3. $Q-K1$	$B-QKt4$	10. $Q-QR1$	$B-KKt5$
4. $Q-QB1$	$B-KB8$	11. $Q-KR8\dagger$	$B-KR6$
5. $Q-KB4$	$B-QR3$	12. $Q \times B\dagger$	$B-KR7\dagger$
6. $Q-KKt4$	$B-QKt2$	13. $Q \times B\dagger\dagger$	
7. $Q-Q1$	$B-K5$		

(18) W. Massmann, *Neue Leipziger Zeitung,* 1936. This problem is to be found in a book by F. J. Prokop, *1000 auserlesene Schachaufgaben,* Prague, 1944, no. 423.

(19) Dr. K. Ebersz, *Magyar Sakkvilag,* 1940. The analysis was given by Duchamp and Halberstadt in *L'Opposition et les cases conjuguées,* Paris and Brussels, Lancel & Legrand, 1930, p. 111, no. 244. Torres y Quevedo constructed an automaton that, by means of the king and the rook, gives mate to the king, moved by a living partner, from an arbitrary initial position in the minimum number of moves; *Scientific American Supplement* 6 (1915), p. 296. The invention of electronic devices, such as those utilized in modern computing machines, makes it possible to imagine automata performing even more complicated tasks. (See *Cybernetics* by N. Wiener, Wiley, New York, 1948).

(21) This game is said to have been invented by the famous Sam Loyd. The theory of the game was given by W. Johnson and W. E. Story in *American Journal of Mathematics* 2 (1879), pp. 397-404.

(23-25) E. Zermelo: 'Uber eine Anwendung der Mengenlehre auf die Theorie des Schach-spiels,' *Proceedings of the Fifth International Congress of Mathematicians,* Cambridge, 1912, Vol. 2, pp. 501-4. H. Steinhaus, 'Games, an informal talk,' *American Mathematical Monthly* 72 (May, 1965), pp. 457-468.

(26) In 1917 Fauquenbergue established that the number $2^{127}-1$ is a prime. D. H. Lehmer devised a machine on a photoelectric basis that examines the divisibility of giant numbers; it was exhibited in 1933 at the Century of Progress Exhibition in Chicago. Since that time great progress in computing machines has been achieved by electronic devices. Cf. article by J. E. Littlewood about large numbers, in *Math. Gazette* 32 (1948), pp. 163-71; J. C. P. Miller and D. J. Wheeler, *Nature* 168 (1951), p. 838; H. S. Uhler, *Scripta Mathematica* 18 (1952), pp. 122-31. It is no longer possible to assess adequately the changes brought about by the application of computers to all of science. Donald B. Gillies, Three new Mersenne Primes, *Mathematics of Computation* 18 (1964), p. 93.

(28) H. Kowarzyk, H. Steinhaus, S. Szymaniec, 'Arrangement of chromosomes II,' *Bull. Acad. Pol. Sc. VI* 14 (1966), pp. 401-4.

(29) H. Iwaniszewski, 'Stellar magnitude in the Aquila field,' *Stud. Soc. Sc. Torunensis,* F., Vol. 1, p. 64.

(31) W. W. Rouse Ball, *Mathematical Recreations and Essays,* London, Macmillan & Co., 1939, pp. 165 and 171. Also Ahrens, op. cit. pp. 255 and 293.

(32, 33) A. Hulanicki, when a student at the University of Wroclaw, found an easy proof of the theorem about the 'prohibited' fields, which has been published in *Wiadomości Matematyczne.*

(33) Dudeney, op. cit. pp. 102-3; Ahrens, op. cit. p. 381. The knight's tour was composed by a Russian officer, Jaenisch; *Chess Monthly,* 1859.

(34) Leonhard Euler (1707-83) of Basle was the author of several hundred papers touching almost all domains of higher and of elementary mathematics. The impossibility of arranging 36 officers was proved by Tarry, *Assoc. Fr. Avanc. Sc.,* 1900. See also Bruck and Ryser, *Canadian Journal of Math.* 1 (1949), pp. 88-93. E. T. Parker, "Orthogonal Latin squares," *American Mathematical Society Notices,* Vol. 6, No. 3, June 1959, p. 276. R. C. Bose, S. S. Shrikhande and E. T. Parker, "Further results on the construction of mutually orthogonal Latin squares and the falsity of Euler's conjecture," *Canadian Jour. Math.* 12 (1960), p. 189.

(35) R. A. Fisher, *The Design of Experiments,* Edinburgh, 1947.

(36) B. Gleichgewicht, J. Kucharczyk, H. Steinhaus, *Applicationes Mathematicae* 5 (1960), pp. 21-33.

(38) Socrates' pupil, Plato (429-348 B.C.), discusses the irrationality of $\sqrt{2}$ and of other numbers. The reader may consult the book by Richard Courant and Herbert Robbins, *What Is Mathematics?* Oxford University Press, 1946, ch. 2, §2.

(41) Blaise Pascal (1623-62), geometer and philosopher, discoverer of the barometer, the calculating machine, and the calculus of probabilities, applied mathematical induction in his *Traité du triangle arithmétique* (1665). F. Maurolico (1494-1575) was his predecessor in this method (1575) but his work has been forgotten.

(42) There is a pile of sealed envelopes. Each one contains a note with the following order: Open the next envelope, read the order and carry it out! On the topmost envelope one reads the following order: Open the next envelope, read the order and carry it out! The principle of mathematical induction says: If somebody is resolved to obey the order written on the first envelope, he is compelled to open all envelopes.

(43) Lord Rayleigh, *The Theory of Sound,* London, 1894-96. L. Euler (see *n.* 34) treated the problem of the musical scale and called attention to the fact that, the smaller are the numbers that show the ratio of vibrations, the better are the concords. Claudius Ptolemy (Alexandria, 140 B.C.) assumed as the starting point, besides the eighth, the fifth, and fourth, also the major third 5:4, and constructed a diatonic scale of intervals: 9/8, 10/9, 16/15, 9/8, 10/9, 9/8, 16/15. Here all the concords, together with the minor third, are expressed by numbers below ten, but the seconds vary: once 9/8, the other time 10/9. On a piano so tuned, a melody in C major would sound otherwise than in D major. The tempered scale was introduced by the organist Andreas Werckmeister in 1691.

(45) J. Mikusinski examined the possibility of improving the musical scale, *Problemy* 1954. *Problemy* 10 (103) 1959, pp. 668-75.

(46) A. Zeising (1854) in his book *Neue Lehre von den Proportionen des menschilchen Körpers* attributes an exaggerated significance to the golden section.

(47) L. Fibonacci lived in Pisa about 1200. The idea visualized by the tree has been suggested by an article of E. Żyliński in the reports of the *International Mathematical Congress* in Bologna 4 (1928), pp. 153-56. (See also *Acta Soc. Botanicorum Poloniae* 5 (1928), pp. 380-91, in which the so-called Ludwig's Law or the role of Fibonacci's numbers in botany is discussed by D. Szymkiewicz.)

(48) Palazzo della Cancellaria in Rome.

(50, 51, 52, 53, 54) In **(51)** the area surveyed by C is one-eighth of the whole pasture;

299

in **(52)** it is already 1/4; the point at which the three areas meet has 1/2, 5/8 as co-ordinates if (0,0) and (1,1) are the opposite corners of the pasture; in **(53)** the common point is 1/2, 13/24; in **(54)** the longest ride of A is $\sqrt{505}/48$, of C $\sqrt{601}/48$, the common point being the same as in **(53)**. Mr. Leon Bankoff from Los Angeles proposes in *The American Math. Monthly* 59 (Nov. 1952), pp. 634-35, another solution: Let the triangle ABC be equilateral; the prolongations of the three heights (from the middle of the sides) divide the square into three equal parts, each of them being entrusted to another cowboy (we begin the construction with the auxiliary segment *pq* dividing the square into two rectangles at the ratio 2:1; and pass through the points marking the first and the third quarters of this line straight lines, each of which makes with the line *pq* an angle of 30°, eventually finding

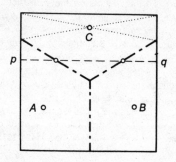

point C as the intersection point of the dotted lines). In this partition: (I) the areas are equal, (II) the maximum rides are equal, (III) each pasture point is entrusted to the nearest cowboy; but principle (IV) to place every cowboy in a point which minimizes his longest ride, is not respected. Among our five solutions, only the first, i.e. **(50)**, has all four advantages I-IV. **(51)** has II and IV; **(52)** II, III, and IV; **(53)** has I, II, and IV; while **(54)** possesses only I and III. Mr. L. Bankoff considers his solution as an improvement of division **(50)**, because it yields shorter maximum rides than **(50)**. But this is not an answer to the query if among all partitions fulfilling all the conditions I-IV, solution **(50)** yields the shortest maximum rides or not. Does the reader grasp the problem posed? See also *Amer. Math. Monthly* 65 (Dec. 1958), p. 775.

(56) J. Schreier, *Mathesis Polska* 7 (1932), pp. 154-60.

(59) [x] means here the greatest integer not surpassing x. Thus [5.7], for instance, means 5, [6] means 6.

(61) C. A. B. Smith, 'The counterfeit coin problem.' *The Mathematical Gazette* 31 (1947), no. 293, pp. 31-39. Blanche Descartes found a simpler method (*Eureka*, no. 13, Oct. 1950). A. M. Rusiecki devised a new method of discovering forged coins by means of three weighings when it is known that among 14 coins one is forged (heavier or lighter than the others remaining) and it is not 0. Each time we place 5 coins on the weighing scale:

$$a = (0, 6, 8, 10, 12) - (5, 7, 9, 11, 13),$$
$$b = (2, 4, 5, 7, 12) - (0, 3, 6, 11, 13),$$
$$c = (0, 4, 5, 10, 11) - (1, 2, 7, 8, 13).$$

We set a, b, c equal to +1 if the left scale is heavier, −1 if the right scale is heavier, finally 0 if both scales are in equilibrium. We then compute: $n = (9a + 3b + c)(-1)^{a+b+c}$

If $n > 0$ then n designates the number of the coin which is heavier than the others, if $n < 0$, $-n$ is the number of the coin which is lighter than the others.

(62) M. C. K. Tweedie, in *The Mathematical Gazette* 23 (1938), pp. 278-82, has given a graphical solution of the wine problem; our picture is a modification of his idea.

(63, 64) This has been noticed by H. Auerbach and S. Mazur.

(65) B. Knaster and H. Steinhaus, *Ann. de la Soc. Polonaise de Mathématiques* 19 (1946), pp. 228-31. H. Steinhaus, *Econometrica* 16 (1948), pp. 101-4.

(68) A fair division into three parts was discovered by G. Krochmalny in Berdechów in 1944. When informed of this, Mrs. L. Kott found another solution. No publication was possible.

(69) G. Pólya, *L'Enseignement mathématique* 4 (1919), pp. 355-79. The property of an equilateral triangle that the sum of distances from its sides is a constant is a theorem of Viviani. The change in direction of the arrow corresponds to the assumption that the first polling gives a point in the cell (1, 2, 2), which lies higher than the point lying in the cell (2, 2, 1) obtained at the second polling. Now party A would lose votes and gain a seat, contrary to what has been said in the text. The solution of this difficulty: We said that it is impossible for a party gaining votes to lose a seat to the advantage of a party losing votes, but we did not say that a party losing votes could gain no seat. The inverted arrow means that party A gains a seat lost by party C, which, too, has lost votes. This is in no way a contradiction: A party can, in spite of losing votes, gain a seat, namely the seat of another party which, too, has lost votes.

(71) Cf. Note **(3)** and H. Weyl, *Symmetry,* Princeton University Press, 1952.

(100) This questions is like those of Chapter 12. It was proposed by the author to his students and answered by K. Florek, T. Dorozeinski, and J. Reszka.

(101, 102) The principle of a slide rule was given by E. Gunter in 1623. In 1671 S. Partridge designed an instrument similar to our present slide rule. If the product appears beyond the scales, we must place the number 10 (instead of 1) opposite the multiplier.

(103) The nomography was discovered by two French mathematicians; Massau and M. P. Ocagne (1889).

(104) The law of the lens was discovered in 1693 by Edmund Halley, the famous English astronomer (1656-1724).

(106) The Minorite Marin Mersenne (1588-1648) arrived at the formula showing the number of vibrations of a string tensely stretched by way of experiment. The formula is valid for the units centimeter-gram-second; if the power P is given in English units, it must be multiplied by 981 cm/sec^2 before being put into the formula.

(107) G. Pick, *Geometrisches zur Zahlenlehre, Ztschr. d. Vereines 'Lotos,'* Prague, 1899; H. Steinhaus, *'O polu figur płaskich,' Przegląd Mat.-Fiz.,* 1924. How may one formulate the corresponding rule for space? Ivan Niven and H. S. Zuckerman, "Lattice Points and Polygonal Area," *Amer. Math. Monthly* 74 (1967), p. 1195.

(108, 109, 110) H. F. Blichfeldt, *Transactions of the American Mathematical Society* 15 (1914), pp. 227, 235.

(111, 112) M. Warmus, *Colloquium Mathematicum* I, 1 (1947), pp. 45-46.

(112) H. Minkowski, *Geometrie der Zahlen,* Leipzig, Teubner, 1912. Simplified proof: Hilbert and Cohn-Vossen, *Geometry and the Imagination,* Chelsea, New York, 1952. The latter book contains many beautiful diagrams and photographs.

(113) This problem was posed and solved by G. Pólya. We chose a different method of solution.

(115) W. Sierpiński, *Bulletin de l'Académie des Sciences de Cracovie,* A (1912), pp. 462-78. Such curves were first determined by G. Peano, an Italian mathematician.

(121) Schnirelman, *Uspiechy Mat. Nauk,* t. 10 (1944), pp. 34-44. This article had already been published in 1929 in the bulletin of the Mathematical Section of the Communist Academy in Moscow.

(122) H. Steinhaus, *Mitteilungen der Sächsischen Akad.* 82 (1930), pp. 120-30. *Przegląd Geogr.* 21 (1947) brings a notice by the same author where the average declivity g of a district is defined by $\tan g = h\Sigma L_i/B$; B is the area of the district, h the vertical distance of two consecutive levels, L_i the length of the i-th level. Cf. an article by the same author in the *Comptes Rendus de la Soc. des Sciences et des Lettres de Wrocław,* série B, 1949, where the length of order n is defined so as to be applied to geographical questions.

(130, 131) The Italian geometer L. Cremona and the English physicist James Clerk Maxwell devised, about 1875, the 'graphical statics' based on the principle of reciprocal figures. Thanks to this method the calculation of steel construction has been simplified. Eiffel, the constructor of the 300-meter tower, applied graphical statics.

(132) H. Steinhaus, 'A bridge with a hexagonal framework,' *Zastosowania Matematyki* 6 (1967), pp. 333-39.

(135-137) I. Grochowska, *Polska Akademia Umiejętności Wydawnictwa Śląskie, Prace Biologiczne,* no. 2 (1950), pp. 1-72. These studies of Hepaticae in the Silesian Beskid include an English summary. W. Steslicka-Mydlarska, *Ann. Uniw. M.C.-S Sectio C:* II, 2 (1947), pp. 37-109 & I-VIII. This method is the work of the Applied Section of the Polish Mathematical Institute and is called 'the Wrocław taxonomy.'

(138) Apollonius of Perga (*fl.* 247-205 B.C.) studied the properties of conic sections.

(140) M. Warmus, *Ann. de la Soc. Polonaise de Mathématique* 19 (1946), pp. 233-34, without proof.

(141) A. Zieba gave this solution without proof.

(144) René Descartes, the inventor of analytic geometry, mentions this spiral in a letter to Mersenne in 1638. The logarithmic spiral appears in nature when an organism grows in such a manner that it keeps its similitude to the shape it had in any previous stage. Cf. D'Arcy W. Thompson, *Science and the Classics,* Oxford University Press, 1940, pp. 114-47.

(145) The equation of this spiral is $r = ae^{c\Phi}$ (where $e = 2.71828\ldots$, $c = 0.274411\ldots$, a arbitrary), r being the distance from vertex and Φ the angle against a fixed direction. The ship's course makes an angle of $74°39'12''$ with the line from ship to vertex.

(150) Archimedes (287-212 B.C.), one of the greatest mathematicians of all time, calculated the ratio of the circumference of a circle to its diameter correct to the third decimal point; he discovered the laws of floating bodies and the beginnings of higher mathematics. Cf. W. W. Rouse Ball, *A Primer of the History of Mathematics,* 4th edition, Macmillan & Co., London, 1895.

(151) Henry T. Brown, *507 Mouvements mécaniques,* Liège, Desoer, p. 28, nos. 96, 97.

(153) Peaucellier, a French naval officer, discovered this linkage in 1864. He was anticipated by Sarrus *(Comptes Rendus de l'Académie de Paris* 36 (1853), p. 1036), who approached the problem from a different side.

(156) L. Mascheroni, *Geometria del compasso,* Pavia, 1797. Napoleon I studied this book. Georg Mohr *(Euclides Danicus,* Amsterdam, 1672), who anticipated Mascheroni in constructions with the compass alone, has been forgotten. Cf. Courant and Robbins, op. cit., ch. III, pp. 147-52.

(157) H. Rademacher and O. Toeplitz, *The Enjoyment of Mathematics,* Princeton University Press (1957), p. 204.

(158) Adam Kochański, a Polish Jesuit, published this construction in *Acta Eruditorum* in 1685. He was the first to utilize a steel spring for suspension of the pendulum of a clock.

(160) Cf. A. H. Stone and J. W. Tukey on generalized 'sandwich' theorems in *Duke Math. Journal* 9 (1942) pp. 356-59, and H. Steinhaus, *Fundamenta Mathematicae* 33 (1945), pp. 245-63.

(162) Nicholas Copernicus (1473-1543), the great astronomer, proved that the planets are circling around the sun and that the earth obeys this law too. His work, *De revolutionibus orbium coelestium,* appeared in 1543.

(165) John Bernoulli, one of the creators of higher mathematics, born in 1667, presented in 1696 the problem of the brachistochrone or the line of quickest fall, and solved it in the year following. The angular velocity ω of the wheel, its radius r, and the acceleration g of gravity are connected by $g = r\omega^2$.

(170) Immanuel Kant, the great German philosopher (1724-1804).

(171) Courant and Robbins, op. cit., ch. VII, §8.

(173) Rademacher and Toeplitz, op. cit.

(175) A problem proposed to college students in Russia. *Uspiechi Mat. Nauk,* 3 (1948), no. 2 (24), p. 239.

The lens shape, though maintaining contact, cannot roll without slipping, because the length of its curved side is not equal to the length of the side of the triangle. Michael Goldberg, "Circular-arc Rotors in Regular Polygons," *American Mathematical Monthly,* Vol. 55 (1948), pp. 392-402; "Two-lobed Rotors with Three-lobed Stators," *Journal of Mechanisms,* Vol. 3 (1968), pp. 55-60.

(176) Motors with rotating pistons, invented by Felix Wankel, have been developed in Germany and in the U.S.A.

The curve (176) is described by the point (x,y) when $x = \cos t + 0.1 \cos 3t$, $y = \sin t + 0.1 \sin 3t$, t varying from 0° to 360°. There are non-circular convex curves with inscribed invariable rotating squares.

(179) K. Zindler ('Uber konvexe Gebilde, ii,' in *Monatshefte f. Math. u. Phys.* 31 (1921), pp. 25-29) noticed that there were noncentral curves whose chords halving the circumference also halve the area. H. Auerbach, 'Sur un problème de M. Ulam concernant l'équilibre des corps flottants,' in *Studia Mathematica* 7 (1938), pp. 121-22.

(180) Cf. note (41). Nicomedes lived about 200 B.C.

(183) Rademacher and Toeplitz, op. cit.

(184) Painting by Bernardino Pinturicchio (1454-1513) representing *The Return of Ulysses* (National Gallery, London); authorized reproduction.

(187) H. Steinhaus, 'Sur la localisation au moyen des rayons X,' *Comptes Rendus de l'Académie des Sciences* 206, May 1938, pp. 1473-75. Cf. U.S. Patent Office nos. 2,441,-538, 11 May 1958: Method of and apparatus for localizing foreign bodies.

(193, 194) Invented by J. G. Mikusinski.

(199) K. W. Pohlke discovered this theorem in 1858 and published it in 1860 without giving the proof. The elementary proof was given by H. A. Schwarz in the *Journal f. reine u. angewandte Mathematik* 63 (1864), pp. 309-14.

(204) If we turn such a model quickly, we see black lines of an unexpected course. These are the points of apparent intersections of the edges moving along.

(211) The model has been invented by Mr. C. H. Dowker and Mrs. Y. N. Dowker of the University of London.

(224) M. Brückner, *Vielecke und Vielflache,* Leipzig, 1900, p. 130. The cosine of the acute angle of the rhombus is 1/3.

(227-232) Weyl, op. cit.

(233-255) Cf. *n.* **(38).** The volumes of the five regular solids of the edge *a* are: $a^3 \sqrt{2}/12$, a^3, $a^3 \sqrt{2}/3$, $a^3(15 + 7 \sqrt{5})/4$, $5a^3(3 + \sqrt{5})/12$. See H. S. M. Coxeter, *Regular Polytopes*, New York, 1949, p. 22.

(263) The faces of this dodecahedron cannot be *regular* pentagons, because of the crystallographic restriction. See Coxeter, op. cit. p. 63.

(267) Ibid. p. 69.

(273) Ibid. p. 96.

(277) The picture of the moon (inverted in the telescope) was taken by the Paris Observatory on 26 April 1898 at 7:09 p.m.

(278) A remark by M. Warmus.

(280) G. Mercator (1512-94). There are no projections preserving lengths unaltered.

(287-290) R. Nowakowski found the third cone. Miss Zenobia Mazur found many more cones, for instance, cones with a triangularly shaped tessellation **(74)** or such that arose by putting together two quadratically shaped tessellations. *Matematyka* no. 1 (29), 1954.

(296) The equation of this curve is $y = a \sin bx$. The function 'sine' was introduced in the second century after Christ by the Alexandrian astronomer Ptolemy.

(307) This electrocardiogram was taken by Prof. H. Kowarzyk of the Medical Academy in Wroclaw; he is the inventor of the apparatus alluded to in **(308)**.

(309) This rule requires a commentary. Assuming an ordinary gait, one has to limit his outlook; stormy weather excepted, experiments on the Baltic seacoast were satisfactory when the walker limited his view to the next hundred yards.

(310) Cf. note (138).

(313) The laws of the revolution of planets were discovered in 1609 by J. Kepler (1571-1630).

(320) If *(a:b)/(c:d)* has a constant value other than 1, then we shall obtain a hyperbolic paraboloid other than that given by the construction described in the text.

(325) This minimal surface is called a catenoid. Any given contour immersed in soap solution will give us a minimal surface bounded by the contour. (C. V. Boys, 'Soap Bubbles,' *Romance and Science Series,* London, 1924-25; there we also find a recipe for soap suds.)

(326) F. Minding (1806-85) discovered this surface, and F. Beltrami (1935-1900) found that creatures living on such a surface would consider the non-Euclidean geometry of Lobatchevsky, with the sum of angles in a triangle smaller than 180°, as natural. N. Lobatchevsky (1793-1856) and J. Bolyai (1802-60) discovered that there are consistent geometries different from the Euclidean system. (Cf. Courant and Robbins, op. cit. ch. IV, §9.)

(328) Coxeter, op. cit. pp. 5-12.

(333) If one end of the new line is on a given vertex and the other yields a new vertex on an already given line, the *V* would increase by 1 and *S* by 1; *L* would increase by 2 and the formula $V + F = L + 1$ would still be correct. But if both ends of the new line formed two new vertices on already given lines, the *V* would increase by 2, *F* by 1, and *L* by 3 (one new line and parts of two given lines) — and Euler's formula would be valid again. Finally, it may occur that the new line is joined by one of its ends to the limiting net, while the other end terminates in the 'field'; but then the new lines gives no new country and *S* remains unchanged. On the other hand, *V* and *L* increase simultaneously by 1 — in case the new line starts from an old vertex, as on figure **(333)** — or *V* and *L* increase simultaneously by 2 — in case the initial point of the new line lies in a new vertex. In both cases the Eulerian formula remains correct.

(338) Cf. note **(34)**.

(347) J. B. Listing (1808-82) published in 1847 the first book on topology. Cf. Courant and Robbins, op. cit. ch. v. The permanence of knots was proved by H. Schubert, *Sitzungsberichte der Heidelberger Akademie der Wissenschaften, Math.-Naturwiss. Klasse*, 1949, 3. Abhandlung.

(357) A. F. Moebius (1790-1863). The band appears in his *Werke*, vol. 2 (1858), p. 519.

(365) F. Frankl and L. Pontriagin, *Mathematische Annalen* 102 (1930), pp. 785-89.

(366) The four-color problem was proposed by Moebius in 1840. It has been proved for all maps containing less than 35 regions by Philip Franklin, *Journal of Mathematics and Physics* 16 (1937), pp. 172-84. A simple proof of Heawood's theorem that five colors are sufficient for every map is to be found in Courant and Robbins, op. cit. Appendix to ch. v. For an account of the seven-color theorem see J. H. Cadwell, *Topics in Recreational Mathematics* (Cambridge Univ. Press, 1966). Ch. 8.

(373) Proposed by H. Lebesgue in *Mathematische Annalen* 70 (1911), pp. 166ff.; the proof is not sufficient; proved by L. E. J. Brouwer in *Journal f. reine u. angewandte Mathematik* 142 (1913), pp. 150ff.

(374) Proposed by S. Ulam and proved by K. Borsuk in *Fundamenta Mathematicae* 20 (1933), pp. 177-90.

(375) L. E. J. Brouwer.

(378) The law of adiabatics is due to S. D. Poisson (1781-1840). Law of Boyle: 1662.

(380) Cf. note **(41)**. The triangle was known to the Arabs in the 13th century (Omar Khayyam). In Europe G. Cardano wrote of its properties in 1570.

(381) J. G. Smith and A. J. Duncan, *Sampling Statistics and Applications*, New York, McGraw-Hill, 1945, pp. 137-52.

(385) J. B. Trevan, *Proceedings of the Royal Society*, B 101 (1927), p. 483.

(386) A. J. Lotka, *Elements of Physical Biology*, Baltimore, Williams and Wilkins, 1925. He gives the following references: p. 70: H. G. Thornton, *Annual of Applied Biology*, 1922, p. 265; p. 74: H. S. Reed and R. H. Holland, *Proceedings of the National Academy of Sciences*, 5 (1919), p. 140; p. 360: *American Reference Book*, 1914, p. 235, *World Almanac*, 1921, p. 277; *Statistical Abstracts*, 1920, p. 814; p. 103: *Tables of Glover*. Using the works referred to above, Lotka calculated the functions; our drawings are based on his data.

(389) F. E. Croxton and D. J. Cowden, *Applied General Statistics*, New York, Prentice-Hall, 1946, ch. 16, pp. 452-58; Chart 171, p. 457. The logistic curve was discovered by the Belgian mathematician, Verhulst. Cf. Raymond Pearl, *The Biology of Population Growth*, New York, A. A. Knopf, 1925, ch. XVIII.

Index